BFF ENDORSEMENTS

*"Hallelujah!
Warm and witty,
Garrett Miller bestows illumination.
Amen!"*
Jeff Michaels
Author
www.JeffreyJMichaels.com

*"Witty life-lessons from Garrett Miller, a man who should be doing stand up!
His fresh cup of honesty is delicious."*
Craig Campobasso
Casting Director and Author
www.CraigCampobasso.com

"Garrett Miller is one of the most intoxicatingly optimistic people on the planet, and his debut book reflects this. I dare you to read it and not feel your heart lighten. It's the perfect read for when you're convinced that the world is horrible and there's nothing you can do about it--there's a lot you can do, starting with changing your attitude!"
Gayle Carline
Humor Columnist, Mystery Author
www.GayleCarline.com

The Blond Jesus-*Isms*
10 Inspired Stories of Miracles and Strength

Garrett Miller

Universal Kingdom Print

Los Angeles • New York • London

This edition first published in 2017
© 2017 Garrett Miller

Universal Kingdom Print of RJTIO
Published by Universal Kingdom Print
United States of America
10 9 8 7 6 5 4 3 2 1

For details on our global editorial offices, customer service, and information about applying for permission to reuse the copyright material in this book, see our website www.universalkingdominternational.com

All rights reserved. No part of this book may be reproduced, scanned, or distributed in any printed or electronic form without permission.

The publisher is not associated with any product or vendor mentioned in this book and does not have any control over nor assumes any responsibility for errors issues that occur after publication due to any such mentioned agendas. The publication is sold on the understanding that all brand names used in this book are trade names, service marks, trademarks, or registered trademarks of their respective owner.

Many Universal Kingdom Print books are available at special quantity discounts for bulk purchase. For details, contact the author, author's official representative, or publisher.

Publishing editor: RJ Tolson

ISBN-13: 978-0996930116
ISBN: 0996930116
Universal Kingdom Print

THE BLOND JESUS-ISMS

1) Don't Be A Dick

2) Fan Club, Party of 1

3) You Get Extra Points with Spinach

4) Wear Rubbers Hiking The Whoa-Ez-Me Trail of Tears

5) Oh Hell Yeah!

6) You're Stuck With Me, Doesn't Mean Forever

7) Starving Your Spirit on Pizza and Beer Does Not A Model Make

8) Hanging Out at the Suckerberg's Cliff of Lemmings

9) I'm Going To Rule The World When I Grow Up

10) Guess What? It's Going To Be Ok

FOREWARD

"Life is not fair. Karma is not absolute. Someone could hurt you deeply, and yes get away with it. You will make mistakes, but if you focus on them you will never be free. Life will give you 1 million chances to succeed ......But you're the one that's going to have to keep putting 1 foot in front of the other. Stop making fun of others....... it shows how little class you truly have."

The above statements are what I learned from reading Garrett's book. There's so much more here, written in a comical, whimsical, and in-your-face way that can help you move from where you are right now to where you'd really like to be.

I loved reading this book. I love his honesty. I love how Garrett is willing to call himself out, as he recalls his failures in life... As well as his successes.

If you don't find yourself in one of these chapters. it just simply means your dead. Don't worry about it. Because your dead, there's no reason to worry. Stay on your fluffy cloud up above looking down at us ridiculous humans, and enjoy the view.

I guarantee that if you're honest, you're going

to find yourself somewhere in this book. You will notice maybe an insecurity that you recognize due to Garrett's insightful writings. Or maybe you'll notice compassion. Or maybe you'll notice, like me, a tear drifting down your cheek... As you read about the boy who is dumped from his high school dance by a pretty girl two days before the event... Yes that's correct two days before the event, so that she could go with someone more popular.

I loved Garrett's connection to his own emotions. To human emotions. We need more books like this, to help us to look at the truth of who we are. To look for compassion. Understanding. Acceptance. For ourselves, as well as those around us.

When Garrett Miller invited me to be on his radio show, we were connected by a mutual friend who lives part-time in California and part-time in South America. From the minute the show opened I knew we would have a blast. Even though Garrett is a positive thinker, he loved the principles that I set out in my number one best-selling book about the myth of positive thinking. The show was filled with laughter from both of our sides, as well as stories about how to get the most out of life. I love stories. Garrett Miller, in this incredible book, shares story upon story that will help you to feel more connected to yourself and to this world.

And what more could you ask from a book, than to bring you closer to your own self, and at the same time open your heart to be more accepting and loving to those around you. I applaud Garrett for his beautiful work here, and encourage him to never stop writing."

David Essel, M. S., Counselor, Master Life Coach and number one best-selling author of "Positive thinking will never change your life....But this book will! The myth of positive thinking, the reality of success"

www.DavidEssel.com

BLOND JESUS-ISM #1

Don't Be A Dick

THE ISM OF 1:

There's a time and a place for everything. And now's the time you want to whip out your dick? Think before dicking.

PALPABLE PARABLE:

Growing up your parents told you, and you believed them, that you were the most handsome boy, or the prettiest girl, the smartest in your class, most gifted athlete, best singer, brilliant artist, bendiest gymnast, master debater, dog whispering, kiss stealin' wheelin' dealin' jet flyin' limosine ridin' son of a gun. Or daughter of a gun. Or however you were identified. You're special. You're unique. You know, just like everybody else.

Fast forward to your present day. Real world. You've settled into your corporate stooge job while secretly believing the "suspension of disbelief" your parents pounded into your psyche all those years ago. "Yes, I'm the single best thing to hit this planet since the invention of sliced bread! It must be true! My parents would never lie to me!"

"Well, there was the deal with Santa Clause."

"And, well, ok, just because rabbits don't lay plastic chicken eggs filled with orange flavored jelly beans, doesn't mean there isn't an Easter Bunny who didn't leave a hollow chocolate bunny in a colorful basket for me to eat right before going to church for the first time since Christmas."

Take a breath for Christ's sake.

Contrary to popular present-day beliefs, not every kid is special. Not every kid is a winner. Not everyone deserves to get a trophy at the end of the season with their gluten-free, dairy-free, sugar-free, nut-free, GMO-free snack de jour.

There are lots of losers in life. Statistically, this has been proven true time and again. At one point, chances are you have been a loser, too. You probably also know some losers. I've also been a loser - lots of times, too. Remember, we are in this together. And it will be ok.

Back to the winners... Do you know who the winner of your group is? Look at your circle and if you can't find the winner, then you're it. Congratulations!

Here, let me get you that trophy from 3rd grade. Your mom still has it on the mantle to show off every Sunday night when you take your picture-perfect family over to your parent's picture-perfect home for your picture-perfect award-winning roast beef Normal Rockwell family dinner that never ever happens. Not even on Fantasy Island.

So if it's not about the trophy, then what does being a winner really mean?

In this book, I'm diving into my ideas of winning concepts of what winners looks like, what winners do, who winners are, and why being a winner is the most important thing you can ever choose to do.

Besides, being a winner is fun!

But make no mistake about winners. Being a

winner does not entitle you to be a dick at any time. Winners do not make others feel small. Winners elevate others in life. Winners aren't corporate snake oil scammers who cheat hard working people from a living wage. Winners are people we can easily admire, respect, and who do what is right – even when they think nobody is watching.

We're always watching.

Winners are Winners.

Winners are *not* dicks.

FORTUITOUS FABLE:

I see winners everywhere. In fact, I'm surprised when I run into dicks. In my world you just don't rise to the occasion, so to speak, if you're a dick.

The following is a true story.

In 2012, I started hosting a radio show five nights a week, fifty weeks a year. Now, with over 1,000 episodes of original content in the rearview mirror, the show pretty much runs itself. **Rated G Radio** is, by far, the most enjoyable thing I do. I get to make new friends from around the world every night, and I always learn something new. I am lucky. There's a wide range of interesting guests lining up months in advance ready to talk about their latest movies, TV shows, cd's, books or other passion projects.

Totally cool, right? Absolutely!

I'm often asked about the guests and what they're like behind the scenes. My guests are generous, kind, gracious, fun, engaging and often they are great storytellers. Perfect for radio. These guests have likely done hundreds of media appearances in the past and they "get it." Be a professional.

From 6-time Emmy winner, Janette Barber; Parks & Recreation television star Jim O'Heir; to multi-Grammy award winning singer-songwriter Bunny Sigler; Billboard magazine chart-topping artists like Margo Rey or Nikkole; or #1 best selling authors like David Essel, Gayle Carline or RJ Tolson, they all get it. Hundreds of other entertaining guests have also been on the show who are delightful and surprising. They are easy guests to work with from start to finish. They are welcome back any time. Why? Because they are professional.

Let me give you an example of someone who never made it to the show, and won't ever be a guest because... he is a dick.

In 2014, someone suggested I contact a particular actor to be a guest so he could promote a project he was trying to fund. Everyone was doing a crowd funding campaign at the time, and I'm a big supporter of shining bright lights on indie artists. Typically, these creative souls don't have a big label, studio or sugar daddy behind them to fund an overpaid publicist who simply negotiates a date on a calendar to be on the show. These artists are hungry for press and want opportunities to sell their projects on air or in print. I love all creative indie people. Well, most of them, anyway.

Following up on this "hot rising star," I reached out to Mr. Whipper Snapper and invited him onto the show in a private message on Facebook that went something like this:

"Dear Mr. Whipper Snapper;
Your admirer, Francine Fanatic, wrote me raving about your performance as Mop #5 in the new Mega Mop commercial that's on after the late late late show. Francine mentioned you've got a new project coming up and you'd make a great guest on Rated G Radio. I'd love to have you on to talk about you, your career, your new fundraising project, and anything else that will help elevate awareness of your Whipper Snapper brand. Here's a link to my show. Please let me know if you'd like to set a date."

Several days later Whipper Snapper wrote back with feigned enthusiasm. You could almost hear the yawn in his fingertips as he limply stroked his keys:

"Well, you know, I'm kinda a big deal in Pocatello with all of the attention I'm getting from my family after they saw my riveting performance as Mop #5 on late night TV. In fact, my grandma recorded the commercial on her vcr and she said the next time I visit, she's going to invite the entire bridge club over to watch while I provide behind the scenes frame by frame commentary."

Me:
"That's great to hear! I bet your family is proud that you're such an absorbant Mop! So, back to setting up an interview, I've got these next 4 dates open and I'd love to offer you one to promote your new crowd-funding project. Which date works best for you?"

Whipper Snapper, offered a borderline coma inducing response after a several day delay: "I'm really not sure if any of those dates will work. I'm really busy, you know, mopping floors. Before I agree to do your show, I will need a detailed analysis of your programs demographics by region, and..."

And... that was the last time I corresponded with Mr. Whipper Snapper.

Two years later and you still haven't heard of him. Why? Because Whipper Snapper is a dick. I'm sure he's probably busy mopping up a bucket of sob stories about how people just don't get his art.

THE ISM TO REMEMBER:
People don't like working with people who are dicks.

BLOND JESUS-ISM #1:
Don't Be a Dick!

BLOND JESUS-ISM #2

Fan Club, Party of 1

THE ISM OF 2:

It can be lonely when the President of your Fan Club is the same person who stares blankly at you in the mirror every morning after your shower. Whether by necessity or choice, sometimes we are the only one standing in our corner. Cheer louder.

PALPABLE PARABLE:

Growing up you're encouraged to be polite, fit in, to make friends, eat your vegetables, do your homework, go to church, clean your room, brush your teeth, be nice to your brother, don't cut your sisters bangs to see what they'll look like with "just a trim", take a bath, and get plenty of sleep.

You've done everything you've been told. You've been a perfect child growing up. In fact, you're so perfect your parents bragged about you to their friends, co-workers, and the rest of your extended family.

"Jenny won the science award for building a volcano out of ramen soup and mouthwash all by herself! You should see it when it erupts! You'll eat the noodles, but you'll stay for the minty fresh breath!"

"Billy took top honors last weekend playing guitar with his Van Halen tribute band! We only received 15 noise complaints from the neighbors in the last three months he spent rehearsing after school."

What parent doesn't like to brag on their kids? They'll post pictures from sporting events and scholastic achievements all with smiling mugs showing up on Facebook, to their smartphone, or even the new 3D hologram. For those old-timers with a typewriter, you even get a glowing mention in the ancient practice of letter writing to your Aunt Marilyn in Seattle for the family's annual Christmas update.

Note to self: Next year, the family really needs to get Aunt Marilyn a computer. It's such a hassle writing letters and putting them in the mail. Though you don't' see it, cuz you never visit, Aunt Marilyn proudly displays the annual family newsletter on the fridge and reads it every morning when she's getting the cream for her coffee. She wonders why you don't call more often. You have unlimited minutes.

Now you're in the big leagues. You've been invited to eat with the cool kids at lunch. Pretty soon, you're invited to the cool kids houses for parties, sleepovers and movie nights. It feels really great. You've got more friends than you can shake a stick at, and life is pretty awesome.

Fast forward a couple years, and now you're now a senior and it's prom season. You and your bestie Bernice are both nominated for Prom Queen. Of course, if you're reading this and you're a dude, you and your homeboy Hank are both vying for Prom King. You and Bernice/Hank both really want to win what you know will surely be a crucial life changing popularity contest. If you are named Prom King/Queen, you will be the coolest person ever. EVER. You know, because this never happens at any other school in any other city anywhere else in the country. EVER.

You've taken the pulse of your friends at school. You've talked to everyone you think matters and have asked for their vote. You are sure your teeth whitening strips are going to make you the bright favorite and you'll easily win - while ignoring that Bernice/Hank is equally charming, attractive, and convincing to the same audience.

The big day comes.

You and your date are joined by Bernice/Hank, as your official BFF's, you all agree splitting the cost to rent a limo 4-ways is much more exciting than cramming into your 1993 Toyota Tercel with its oxidized red paint.

As the Fab-4, you agree to dine at the tre-chic Soup-Or-Steak at the mall. You order the fish. Your date orders the chicken. Nobody orders soup or steak. "Mom gave me a Groupon, so we can get dessert! Let's get two, and we can each have a bite! We're all getting along so good! This is such a fun night!" you say grinning ear to ear.

So far. So good.

You make it to the dance and are enjoying the extra attention your friends are heaving upon you. The night just continues to get better. The DJ is playing all the current hits by Taylor Swift, One Direction, and Adele.

Promptly at 9:00 p.m. Principle Poundcake huffs and puffs his way onto the podium and summons the prom court nominees to take center stage. The latest song by Justin Timberlake fades. An electronic drumroll taps in the background.

All of the pretty girls stand with each other giggling, with their perfectly curled hair spritzed to the heavens, carnation corsages pinned without too many pricks into their pretty pastel-colored dresses.

The handsome young men are busy high-fiving one another comparing their ill fitted rent-a-tux, hair slicked with pomade, and battling wafts of Axe body spray on freshly shaved faces, some still sporting tissue paper stuck to now hairless chins.

Principle Poundcake taps the microphone, "Ladies and gentlemen, please put your hands together as we congratulate this year's Prom Queen and King... Bernice and Hank!"

Hormones erupt with wild approval! King Hank and Queen Bernice are crowned and share their first dance as scholastic royalty.

You stand there, completely dazed. "Did he just say Hank and Bernice were King and Queen?" You're sure Principle Poundcake misread the envelope! What just happened? Everyone told you, you'd win! How could this travesty occur? Do we have any hanging chad's to account for?

I need to speak to your supervisor – NOW!

You smile as these thoughts race through your head at 100 miles an hour. You could easily have been at a Hollywood award show with the camera watching your reaction as a "loser." You take your date by the hand and somehow manage to get through the next hour on the dance floor before the evening comes to a close.

Neither of you say a word.

Back in the limo your home is the first stop. Before getting out, you lean over and say to your friends with a genuine smile thinking what you'd like Bernice/Hank to say to you if you'd won, "Congratulations. You both looked so great tonight. I'm so happy for both of you, you make a brilliant King and Queen!"

It might not have been what your inside voice was screaming at you, but you know in your heart, you're still a winner. This was Hank and Bernice's night. You know you will have other opportunities to shine.

Oh, by the way, after you left for the prom, the mailman delivered something for you. Inside on the kitchen counter is an acceptance letter from your first choice of colleges offering you a full ride scholarship.

FORTUITOUS FABLE:

I was 26 and just moved into my first home in Phoenix. When I met the realtor several months prior and she pulled up to the curb, my inside voice screamed, "This is it! This is my dream house!" At the time, it was perfect.

Corner lot, 2,100 square foot ranch house with 4-bedrooms, 2-bathrooms, complete with a sunken living room, dual fireplace, swimming pool with a diving board, and an RV parking pad for the travel trailer I'd never want to own. It was mine. All mine.

I could paint the walls any color I wanted, and I could finally get a dog! The opportunities for home improvement were vast, and HGTV didn't even exist yet! The first major project I was excited to undertake involved wallpaper removal. Specifically, the metallic lime green and orange fern print wallpaper in the master bedroom. Similar fashion retro wallpaper could also be found in every other room of the house. The floor to ceiling drapes hadn't been washed since the house was built. And there was linoleum in the kitchen. Linoleum. Orange, yellow, and brown patterned linoleum. From 1979. This was January 1995.

All of these upcoming projects would be costly, but I would find a way to make them work. Mostly, I planned to use a lot of sweat equity in the process. I could nearly afford to do one or two of the projects – if I watched my pennies. So watching pennies I began.

I recently graduated from Arizona State University with my Bachelor's Degree in Agribusiness. I'd completed coursework towards a Master's Degree, while working 60+ hours a week in a call center. My typical day involved helping customers who heard spokesperson Candace Bergan tell them to dial 10-10-whatever to get an operator for a calling card or collect call. That was me who answered you, or more likely your parents and grandparents!

Life seemed pretty good. In five years I'd finished college, learned how to manage the call center with the least amount of staff for the least amount of customer wait time, wrote a company newsletter, received customer commendations and trained classes on call processing. It was a piece of cake!

I was hungry for pie!

Around this same time I got a call that would forever change my life. Jill Fouts, fellow call center alumni, called one evening to tell me about her new job. She screamed, "This job has YOU written all over it!"

"What, EXACTLY, is this job?" I ask several times. She'd try to explain it but my eyes kept rolling into the back of my head.

Finally she had to break it down into basic terms I could grasp. "Oh, it's like helping people with their telephone services. Like when you use call waiting," she said.

Hold on, I've got another call. Click-Click.

I didn't quite get what it involved, but I did get one thing clearly. The base salary was $38,000 a year, plus commission. I was currently working over 60 hours a week to make just a bit more than $32,000. I've never been a math wizard, but this seemed pretty good. Jill said clearly, "You will make $38,000 and only work 40 hours each week, weekends and holidays off. No overtime."

This was not another hourly job. This was not

an entry-level job. This was a salaried position with real vacation, great benefits and other perks-a-plenty mysteriously called commission. I'd finally get to see my aunts, uncles, and cousins who lived in Phoenix for the holidays, where I'd routinely told them in the past "I can't make it this year. I have to work the holiday – it's triple pay!"

The day I got the offer, I raced home to call my Dad who was living in Eugene, Oregon at the time. Historically, my Dad is my #1 fan and supporter and, frankly, someone I have consistently been able to count on for advice, a shoulder to cry on, financial-aid at other times in my life, and, along the way became a good friend as well.

I'll never forget that phone call as long as I live to my #1 supporter!

"Dad! Guess what? The phone company called and offered me the job I was telling you about. They want me to start June 12th and it pays $38,000 a year! Isn't this great?!"

I fully expected him to jump up and down with me and reaffirm I was the brightest, most awesome son a man could ever have. I remembered the things my parents would tell me growing up, "You can do anything you set your mind to…"

See chapter one about the Kool-Aid parents serve their kids – I gulped its sugary goodness, which probably explained my hyperactivity.

Instead, my Dad calmly said in a matter-of-fact tone, "Are you sure you heard it right? $38,000 seems like a lot of money to pay you to answer a phone."

However, all I *heard* him say listening between the lines was, "You're not worth $38,000 a year. Go back to your hourly job and stop imagining things. You've got a mortgage to pay now."

Of course, my Dad was trying to make sure I had a clear grasp of the offer, that I didn't misunderstand the fine print, and that I didn't end up quitting one job with a respectable company for something that sounded "too good to be true."

Here I was, so excited to share this news with him first and he quickly took the air out of my sail. I wanted say, "Dad, please be excited for me! Tell me how proud you are of me for getting such a rewarding job which values me with a respectable salary! I worked hard to get this job, and the interview process was a bitch! Just say 'WAY TO GO' and enthusiastically mean it!"

We chatted a few minutes more. He wished me well, but he didn't believe my "story." At least not until my first paychecks came validating the offer letter. I even mailed him copies of my paystubs to prove the job was real.

That was the day I realized I needed to be my #1 fan, every day. In what should have been one of my most exciting days of my life up to that point, I realized I was the only one cheering for me. There were no other cheerleaders on the sidelines that day. None.

This would not be the last time my Fan Club numbers would be a single digit, but it was the first time I knew what it felt like. I felt horrible. I felt dumb.

You'll be pleased to know, I went on to achieve President's Club recognition five consecutive years, was consistently in the Top 10 in an office of over 200 consultants, and made no less than $75,000 every year while on desk. In fact, my best year was over $115,000 – for working a 40-hour week where I answered the phone and helped people grow their home-based businesses. I even took my Dad with me to my final President's Club in Santa Fe, NM where he was able to see what all the fuss was all about. We had a great time.

I never did make $38,000 at that job.

THE ISM TO REMEMBER:
Give yourself the validation you need to be a winner. Everyone else is busy with their own life. If anyone else cheers along the way, smile and be grateful while it lasts.

BLOND JESUS-ISM #2:
Fan Club, Party of 1.

BLOND JESUS-ISM #3

You get extra points for spinach.

THE ISM OF 3:
Smiling is one of the best things in life. It makes you feel good. It's nearly impossible to feel bad when you smile. Even if you have spinach in your teeth, smile at everyone everywhere you go. You get extra points for spinach.

PALPABLE PARABLE:

"If you don't turn that frown upside down, your face is going to freeze like that! Do you want to go around for the rest of your life with that frozen sour puss?" Surely this could not be. Yet, at an early age your mother told you this *truth* every time you kicked your heels, stomped your feet and waved your hands in the air like you just didn't care. Years later these same mad skills would win you a spot in the finals on Dancing With The Stars. Today, they earn you a swift swat on your butt, time out in your room – without Nintendo, TV, or access to your computer. You've just entered the Black Hole of punishment. How will you ever survive?

Yet, you do.

Sure there are times you are bound to get upset. When Rhonda Rousey lost her first UFC match. When Paula Abdul left American Idol. When you don't get a 10th free refill of iced tea at the Burger Barn.

Somehow you lived to see another day. *Barely*.

Then when real disappointment enters your life, you find more reasonable reasons to frown. When you suffer your first, second and third major breakup – all in the span of 6 weeks during your junior year of high school. "I'll never find anyone who will love me again – ever!" When a family member, friend or pet dies. When a company you've dedicated the last dozen years to doesn't care about working with you any longer. Or, when your usual 40 mile/90 minute commute on the 405 freeway becomes 3 hours and 48 minutes – for no other reason than it's the 405 and the sun is shining.

We've all had experiences in our lives leaving us without sunshine and unicorns. These are times when you're probably not doing a lot of smiling. That's ok. Thankfully troubling times fade and we have the rest of our life to look forward to. The rest of our life that makes *most* of us smile.

At the office, you've got this one co-worker, Debbie. Debbie Downer. Debbie is your one co-worker that no matter what is going on, she refuses to be happy. Debbie never smiles. For her birthday this year, everyone at the office got together and threw Debbie a surprise birthday party. You even stayed late last night to hang up the colorful streamers. Stan in accounting turned blue from blowing up all 52 balloons (one for each of Debbie's dreary years). Her department chipped in $5 each to get Debbie a spa day to help cheer her up. Everyone, including The Big Boss, sang a rousing rendition of Happy Birthday in the lunchroom. Everyone was happy, except Debbie.

First of all, Debbie didn't like the color of cake frosting – it was flamingo pink. Her favorite color is purple. "They all know that..." she'd mutter under her breath. "The spa day is such a waste – I mean, it's 15 minutes from my house. I'll have to schedule it ahead of time for after work or on a weekend. I bet they won't even have the time I'd want to go. Those paper streamers are making my allergies act up. And why is everyone in the lunchroom? Don't they have jobs to do? We're on a deadline!"

She manages a hollow thank you before curtly returning to her desk where she spends the rest of the day irritated at the flowers her mother sent – they aren't right either. "I likes Pansies, and my mother sent Daisy's. Can't anyone do anything right?!"

Near the end of the day, Marge, Helen and Betty stop by her cubicle and invite Debbie to happy hour to celebrate, "C'mon Debbie, let's party! There's ½ priced buffalo wings and jello shots until 7:00 p.m.! They're even got an 80's cover band doing a mega-mix from Duran Duran!"

Debbie will have none of this nonsense. Instead, she opts to stop at the store on her way home to pick up a low-sodium Salisbury steak microwaveable dinner and a 2-liter bottle of diet soda before returning to her lonely home and her lonely life. Besides, there's a marathon of Murder She Wrote on Netflix she's dying to catch, if her internet isn't acting up again.

Debbie does not smile. Nor does Debbie does *want* to smile. Debbie enjoys finding the raincloud in any silver lining. "Ah-ha! I knew it!" she'll proclaim, about anything and everything. Debbie has chosen to wear her sour puss on her sour mug and it leaves everyone around her feeling like a sweet and sour chicken, minus the sweet and minus the chicken. Just sour.

FORTUITOUS FABLE:

When life looks its worst, one of the hardest things to do is to never let them see you sweat. Always keep your chin held high. Never give them the satisfaction of knowing they've knocked you down and kicked your teeth to the back of your throat. When you're at your darkest moment, it's time to smile bright baby, because nothing pisses off your bullies more than ignoring their attacks on you.

I've never understood why some people get a perverse satisfaction out of seeing others fail. This becomes their happiest moments in life. The times when you'll see them laugh hysterically at misfortune and wish ill for their fellow man. In the same breath, you'll hear them tell other people how much good they do in the world, all of the volunteer work they perform, and how sad they were the day they heard Prince died. "I just can't go on. Too soon. He meant the world to me." Really? The guy was a pop music icon, but to have your life come to a standstill? Can you be *less* dramatic? And, here I was putting on Let's Go Crazy to celebrate Prince's legacy.

Yet these Energy Vampires are in our lives, in one form or another. Smiling only when someone else is suffering misfortune. What drives this behavior? Fear? Insecurity? Not enough bran in their diets? We may never know.

Years ago, I worked in a call center while going to college. It was a great job for going to school – flexible on the hours, great benefits and it paid well. While there, I made several lifelong friends like Crystal Thomas, Sally Sparks, Deanna & Blaine Ballard, Julie Rollins and Don Freeman, to name a few. Both Don and Julie were my supervisors at different times. I'm lucky as they got me "off line" *often* to work on different projects to benefit the center – newsletters, international directories, creating forms – you name it, I would volunteer for it, with a smile.

Eventually, I was spending more time off the phones doing other projects than answering hundreds of customer calls every day. I soon developed a working knowledge of these mysterious new programs called Excel and Word Perfect. Some considered me a suck-up, but I considered my off-line time as building added value to the entire center. I'd also become an AIC (agent-in-charge) for supervisors when they were busy and the agents needed an escalation point for angry customers, or when they were having their crisis-de-jour.

It was a role I was great at, but the center didn't have much of a career path. While a career path wasn't at the top of my list while in college, after I graduated it was. If I stayed with the center, my only real option was to be promoted to a supervisor.

Supervisor turnover at this center was non-existent. In the four years I'd been there, they hadn't hired a new supervisor for at least three. Then one day the strangest thing occurred. The center's new Director made the announcement two new supervisors were going to be hired. Two.

Many of the agents came up throughout the day and gave me their early congratulations. Naturally, the best and most deserving candidate, Garrett Miller, would be the easy selection made by management. Right?!

Inside, I laughed to myself, "They're posting for two, I wonder who ELSE they'll be hiring. I can't wait to get my tiny cubical, so I can manage these people and really impress them with my ability to work 80 hours a week while filling out reams of paperwork showcasing lots of i-dotting and t-crossing!"

I applied for the position. I also knew several other people who were applying. And, being the good co-worker I was, when I saw an opportunity to help, I helped. Even if it was my competition. In this case, my competition was a shy and unorganized newer agent. I knew it would be a situational interview, "Give me a time when – what did you do – how did it turn out" scenario. I shared the infinite wisdom I accumulated in my own situational interviews up to that point (zero, though well-intended). We even role-played to help lessen her anxiety. I mean, really, what did I have to lose? I'm the clear #1 pick! Helping my co-worker showed my leadership skills!

When it came time for my interview I was, admittedly, *okay*. I didn't knock my socks off, but I also knew my record of service within the company. I mean, who gets five years of perfect attendance? I did! Surely that had to count for something. Once the interviews were complete, it was just a matter of time until I'd get the good news. I patiently waited, while the other agents continued to pile on the early congratulations! Then the day came and the promoted names were posted in the office for who was selected.

Guess whose name was **not** on that list? Mine. Guess whose was? Yes, the person I coached on how to interview and answer questions. The second hire was a transfer from another center. Another center?!?! The nerve!

Internally shaken, I sat at the in-charge desk that Tuesday afternoon when three ladies came up to me in tears, "Garrett, this is just not right. This doesn't make any sense. You are the perfect person for this job and..."

"ENOUGH ALREADY!" I screamed inside my head. My face told a different story. I smiled and thanked the ladies for their endorsement, but, I told them, it just wasn't my time. My day would come soon enough. Confidently I knew this to be true.

When soon enough came much sooner than expected two months later, the center posted for an additional two more supervisor positions.

My inside voice beamed loud encouragement once again, "Well, SURELY, this time I'll get one of the two positions. I mean, c'mon! I'm ME! Garrett Miller! AIC extraordinaire!"

Surprisingly, my name was not selected for either of these positions. One of the people promoted was a young man who would bring a small stuffed animal shark toy to his cubicle and play with it between calls. He had also been found sleeping at his workstation on more than one occasion. Clearly, this fine young lad, The Shark Whisperer, was a much better choice to help manage the center than I.

When approached by questioning co-workers I'd unconvincingly suggest, "Look, maybe I'm not supposed to get this because something else better is coming along for me." The truth was, at that moment, I had nothing. Nada. But I smiled and did my job. Anything less would be uncivilized.

I began looking for other jobs – at that point I didn't care what I did, but I knew then I'd never be promoted, and the center no longer had any use for my impressive newsletter writing talents. It was time to get outta Dodge.

Within 3 months I had 2 fantastic job offers, with one ending up being a catalyst for changing my life forever.

I planned my exit carefully and checked the supervisor schedules. My last day would also coincide with The Shark Whisperers schedule. When my shift was up, nervously, I walked into the office, handed him my badge and told him I was not coming back. I half expected an alarm to sound with armed guards preventing me from leaving. "Don't let Miller out of the building! We can't survive without him!"

No alarms. No fanfare. Their world continued to rotate without me.

With over five years of loyal service, I walked out. I smiled a lot that day.

THE ISM OF 3:
Smiling is one of the best things in life. It makes you feel good. It's nearly impossible to feel bad when you smile. Even if you have spinach in your teeth, smile at everyone everywhere you go. You get extra points for spinach.

BLOND JESUS-ISM #3
You get extra points for spinach.

BLOND JESUS-ISM #4

Wear Rubbers Hiking the Whoa-Ez-Me Trail of Tears

THE ISM OF 4:
You're going to wade through a lot of bullshit in life. Wear your rubbers to keep from having it wedge between your toes.

PALPABLE PARABLE:

Curt wondered what would be the straw that broke his camel's back. Would it be the broken promises? Would it be the cheating? Would it be the illegal activities he navigated daily? Or would it be the murder of the founder's mother in the desert that sent him running? He wasn't sure what was going on, but in his gut he knew something wasn't right and something needed to change.

Twenty years earlier was much different for Curt. Fresh out of business school at Arizona State, Curt was living a charmed life. During the day, he was working as a marketing manager at the high-end resort at South Mountain. He'd recently met his boyfriend, Jake, at a popular Wednesday night hangout in Scottsdale, BS West, while dancing on one of the go-go boy podiums. A degree. A good job. A nice apartment. And now a hot new man in his life. Life was perfect for Curt. He hoped it would never change.

Except, there's one thing about life always guaranteed to happen, change.

Within the next eighteen months, the honeymoon was in full swing as Curt and Jake moved into their first apartment together. A nice two-bedroom second-floor unit, which overlooked the swimming pool often decorated with beautiful taning bodies of co-eds grabbing some vitamin-D between classes. The spare bedroom was used more for storage of old comic books and Donna Summer albums in banker boxes, but it gave the couple the veil needed should anyone become to curious about their relationship.

One night while out with friends at a local favorite, The Biz on McDowell Road, they met their opponents in a game of billiards Mary and her wingman Fran. Fran was busy eyeing a cute Betty at the end of the bar most of the night, while Mary soon got down to business. "So, what do you boys do?"

Jake explained he was running a small car stereo business off of Baseline Road called, "CarTunes" featuring a mascot, which had an odd resemblance to the Roadrunner. Curt talked about the real estate office he managed in North Phoenix where the owners were always looking for a get rich quick scheme in the fertile housing market in the Valley of the Sun. Neither job could be considered long-term careers.

"So spill it Mary, what's your story?" Curt asked.

"I'm a small business owner with a big dream! Have you heard of *Mary May I Consignment*? People give me their used furniture and I polish it up, put it in my showroom, sell it for a hefty markup and keep the profit. It's like printing money and I'm the printing press!"

"Sounds pretty good," Jake said with the ideas spinning in his head. "Wish we'd find something like that to get in on."

"Boys, here's my card. Call me up on Monday. I could use a couple of cuties like you around." And with that, Mary hit the 8 ball into the corner pocket, winked at them, reached up to adjust her baseball cap, and walked out to her dusty white Ford pickup truck to drive off into the hot desert night.

The next few years were a blur for Curt. Not long after their initial meeting, Jake was hired to be the President of the company, and Curt's affinity for a balanced checkbook found him as the company's CFO. Soon *Mary May I Consignment* had multiple locations throughout Arizona– it seemed people had lots of used furniture they didn't want to part with at their weekly Saturday morning garage sales. Mary was only too happy to take it off of their hands.

"What do you mean, you'll only give me $100 for that faux Louis the XIV dining table. I paid 10 times that just 2 years ago," the customer would exclaim.

"If you could have sold it yourself, you'd already have sold it," she'd say with snark. "So how's that working out for you?"

Ten minutes later the paperwork would be signed, the table taken back into the Mary's warehouse, and promptly put up for sale the following day for $1,000.

"This is how it's done, boys!" Mary would say in her loud booming voice as she'd count out the cash. "Now, get me more stores! I want to be the next Consignment Queen of the World!"

 "A queen..." Curt chuckled under his breath. "That will be the day...."

Jake and Curt set out on a major mission to transform this bull in a china shop to a family friendly personality fit for Saturday morning television. Hiring image consultants, stylists and etiquette experts all worked quickly to turn Scary Mary, into everybody's favorite Aunt Mary. You know, the Aunt Mary who was going to take loving care of that beat up old sofa that was so hard for you to part with. Her commercials began airing on the local channels and on the popular morning radio programs with the tag line, *"Yes you may, at Mary May*

I." Sales skyrocketed within weeks of the initial campaign. Mary's makeover transformation was a hit with the eager used-furniture buyers of Phoenix.

The holidays came early that year for Jake and Curt when Mary announced she was authorizing a major bonus for both. "You two have worked a Christmas miracle! Sales are up 310%, and we've just opened our 7th store. It's time we think bigger. Like Charlotte. And Portland. And Salt Lake. It's time to make *Mary May I* a household name! Here's your bonus, now get to work!"

Curt eyed Jake with puzzled look. The books were good, but where was she getting this bonus money? Jake just smiled back as if to say, "Don't rock the boat, this is what we've been waiting for."

That was the day everything changed, again.

The search for the right franchisees began in 5 key markets. Finding the right people, the right team, and the right fees to license *Mary May I* became an all-consuming goal for Mary. In front of the camera's Mary was the friendly Aunt Mary who would give you a piece of apple pie ala mode. Behind the scenes, Mary was still scary, barking at Jake and Curt, "Get 'em signed. Get 'em on board! Get their check! Next!"

With her empire growing at record speed, so did Mary's demands on the boys.

"I don't want to hear excuses, get that building done 3 weeks early... or else!"

"I want you to hire my new girlfriend I just met as my Executive Assistant at a hefty salary – and NO I don't care that she can't take dictation, make coffee or type. Get her on the payroll now!"

"Fire that good for nothing assistant, she's worthless! Who hired her anyway? Oh, Curt, I've got a new assistant you're going to hire for me, she'll be here in an hour."

"I need $50,000 in petty cash for a new project I'm working on. No, I'm not going to tell you what it is."

The list of demands and secrets would escalate until finally Curt's conscience could take it no more. "Jake, I don't know about you, but

Mary's latest scheme to get money from new franchisees isn't something I can go along with. I don't feel good about it and I'm not going to take the fall for her when this goes south. You know she'll throw us under the bus."

Sitting poolside, Jake looked across the scenic view from their new their multi-million dollar estate which backed up to the lake in this exclusive gated community. The life they'd built was certainly filled with perks. Neighbors who were local sports legends; new cars every year; fancy first-class extended vacations to exotic destinations. Jake looked over at Curt, "We've gone along this far, what's so bad about Mary's latest idea."

"Jake, you know it's borderline criminal!" Curt said sternly.

"Let me sleep on it," Jake said as he sipped on his margarita.

The following day, Jake and Curt called a meeting with Mary to discuss their decision. Both agreed prior they would have to give it all up – the titles, the big paydays, and the big life that went with it. They would be left with little more than their dignity and honor in tact.

"After all these years and after all I've done for you!" the concrete walls shook as Mary screamed. "You are going to be sorry – get out! Get out NOW! Don't ever come back! You're fired!"

"Too late, Mary, we already quit." Curt and Jake said in unison. They walked out the door and, in fact, never looked back.

Without her dream team of Jake and Curt to navigate and steer her ship, soon *Mary May I* began to take on water in this oasis and quckly sunk. Bankruptcy, the shuttering of Mary's empire and public scrutiny would find this once powerful furniture maven, living a life vastly different from the pinnacle of her success.

FORTUITOUS FABLE:

"That's bullshit!" "What a crock of shit!" "That's some fucked up shit!" "Awe, shit!" I'm not sure why these words ring so loud in my head, but I hear these phrases all the time. Used so often the 'swear' part loses its impact and its just part of the conversation.

I don't get freaked out about shit anymore, because it's all the same shit to me.

A couple careers ago, I was wading through waste deep shit at work where I was stuck at the bottom of a mountain of bureaucratic shit in a massive shit factory. It stunk to the high heavens. It wasn't always so stinky. Enough with this shit already, and on with the story.

Five years earlier it was a different universe. I was one of the company's top sales people, earning multiple President Club awards, accolades-a-plenty, a fiercely loyal client base, and regular perks like box seats to see Janet Jackson in concert when Janet was JANET, and a host of other opportunities afforded to one so valuable to a fertile organization.

But then, I got the call.

"Garrett, we're going to hire a new manager, and I'd like it to be you," Director Darlene Emert said. Keep in mind, Darlene was, and still is, probably one of the coolest people on the entire planet. Getting the opportunity to work for her and "be a manager" was like winning the lottery!

Or so I thought.

I'd just come off my most successful year earning over $115,000 and recently completed training for high-end data products like OC1's and other new "cloud based" services, which were too high up in the clouds for me to really grasp. I weighed the new training I just completed and the accompanying income potential versus the promotion I'd waited five years to achieve. The base salary was *a lot* lower than I'd hoped, but knew with my "Go get 'em" attitude, I could move mountains. I'd potentially earn boatloads of commissions, like I had while 'on desk.'

What could go wrong?!?!

The first day as a manager I was presented with Linda's file. She was gifted to me with a "good luck" pat on the back and instructions to send a "return to work" letter to this employee who didn't want to come back from disability for whatever make believe ailment she claimed. The two days of Labor Relations training I had did not prepare me for this situation.

I sat there thinking, "How am I supposed to get to know my new team, endear myself to them, and have them go from last place in the office to #1, when I have to deal with a deadbeat employee who just want to collect disability?"

That was the first day.

Linda, by the way, eventually did return to the work... for about a month... before telling me she was going out on disability *again* – this time so she could get an elective boob job. "TMI" I told her while handing her the required FMLA paperwork. The weeks passed and once her medical leave was up. Again, she refused to return to work. Turns out, as I'd discover much later, during her boob job disability leave, Linda took an extended vacation and also moved, which was why she didn't come back to work when scheduled – she was on vacation! So while she was out each month, as a sales manager, I had to absorb her sales goal and hopefully the rest of the team would pick up the slack so I could earn commission. Oh to be young and naïve again...

Soon after, Bart, another lazy-assed employee on the team looking for any excuse to get out of doing anything remotely resembling his job was about to be performance-managed out the door. He was clever enough to find a not-so-unique way to avoid doing his job of answering the phone and light typing duties of placing orders and making sales. What happened? Overnight, he developed a nasty case of carpal tunnel syndrome. While working with the union to ensure a fair, equitable and helpful work environment, it was decided he would sit at his desk and read training manuals to rest his wrist. I mean, if you sucked at your job, wouldn't it be a great relief to get retrained on company time to become a more effective and ultimately become successful? Nope. A routine computer security check soon discovered his easy ability to surf porn from his workstation. Lots and lots of porn. Adios, Bart.

Another employee thought it would be hysterical to breach security and access the private records of a top level executive's home phone line and forward it to a sex hotline, and not expect to get caught.

And... I can go on for pages and pages. I wanted to coach these people to new cars and homes! Yet, this was the bullshit I got to wade through every day. I was a manager! My dream had come true!

While dealing with the adult daycare drama, a merger with another company brought in a new senior management team. They came barreling in with sports analogies to loudly communicate the new directives: "110% of objective just isn't good enough – you've got to cross that finish line! Hit it out of the park! Go for a Grand Slam Homerun! You must exceed 120% of your sales goals like a Gold Medal Olympic Athlete! While we're at it, your sales center will immediately stop receiving all sales calls and you'll only get customer calls who want to disconnect their service! You will 'save the sale' and upsell each and every call to a successful victory!"

Yeah, cuz that's going to happen.

Several managers in the office would gather outside at the picnic table away from eavesdropping ears to figure out what was going on. "The writing's on the wall," said one of my peers, CT Brazeal – the most strategic thinker of our group who became our unofficial leader. "We figure out how to turn this ship around, or we're sunk."

Stunned, I sat next to my peers who were all equally at a loss for words.

Soon we were summoned to participate in what I affectionately called the "Nightly Beatings." A typical day would start at 6:00 a.m. when I'd show up bright eyed and bushy tailed to open the office, spend the day putting out personnel fires, calming irate customers, trying to coach the few stars I had among the lumps of oatmeal, and then at 6:00 p.m. when the office closed, slink downstairs with the rest of our management team to our 5th floor training room. We'd collapse into our chairs and wait for a national conference call to roar into the room with every call center in the country. We'd be called upon and report why we only sold "x" numbers of packages, cell phones, internet, etc...

The calls usually lasted an hour.

Sometimes longer.

The calls always ended the same. "Tomorrow, you better make up for slacking off with your pitiful sales of 116%. If you don't make it up, there will be hell to pay." Most of the time, our office was the only office in the entire country meeting or exceeding our widget goals. This was not good enough, however.

The collective mindset silently mumbled, "Way to keep us excited about our jobs! We were doing our best with the shitty set of circumstances you've shoveled our way, trying to make this shit shine." Say that five times fast.

One of the senior leaders, I called "Aunt Kate" because of her *oh so warm and fuzzy* personality. Aunt Kate would lead these Nightly Beatings.

"I can't wait for Aunt Kate to come back to Phoenix again! I'm going to bake her chocolate chip cookies and rub her feet!" I'd tell my peers to help lighten the mood. They would laugh, but not too loudly, in case the room was bugged. If it would have cut us some slack, I'd have done it. Everyone hated Aunt Kate. I'm sure she probably hated us too, but how else would she get her million-dollar bonus if the beatings didn't continue?   The stock value post-merger dropping from $60 to $5 certainly wasn't going to do it!

When Aunt Kate came to town, she was prepared. She'd show up all fakey-fake with her fire breathing freshly dyed fire engine red crew cut and accompanying riding crop. Smashing it on the conference table, she'd bark orders to convert every disconnection request into at least one new phone line, and we were losers if we didn't do it. The senior trainers even provided us dialogue to support the bullshit.

We all smelt it, felt it and we were dealt it. It was more bullshit.

Throughout this exciting time, I somehow managed to coach my team from 10th to 2nd place in the office. That was the good news. The bad news, in order to cope with the hours, the beatings and the dark tunnel I was in, I began taking prescription anti-anxiety medications. I also started drinking heavily after work, and felt horrible pretty much every single day. The action of simply getting out of the car and walking into the building 30 yards away started my body sweating profusely. It was gross. "Just 13 more hours and you can go home," I'd tell myself 5 days a week.

Realizing things were going on behind the scenes that I had no control over, I knew I needed to leave with what little sanity I had left. I'd seen this writing before. It took 4 months of careful negotiation before I received an attractive severance package. I even held a Retirement Party with all of my friends and joked about my early release from the shit shack. It was an awesome party. I never looked back.

THE ISM TO REMEMBER:
You're going to wade through a lot of bullshit in life. Wear your rubbers to keep from having it wedge bewteen your toes.

BLOND JESUS-ISM #4:
Wear Rubbers Hiking the Whoa-Ez-Me Trail of Tears

BLOND JESUS-ISM #5

Oh Hell Yeah!

THE ISM OF 5:
If you spend your time saying, "Oh Hell no...!"
It's time for you to go, go, go!

PALPABLE PARABLE:

It's 4:30 a.m. Monday morning. The alarm clock goes off to start another exciting week and the radio's blasting Dolly Parton's, "9 to 5."

"Tumble outta bed and I stumble to the kitchen
Pour myself a cup of ambition
Yawn and stretch and try to come to life
Jump in the shower and the blood starts pumpin'
Out on the street the traffic starts jumpin'
With folks like me on the job from 9 to 5"

You look over to the bedroom window – the blinds can't hide that the sun won't be up for another two hours this time of year. You toss your right leg off the bed, groan as you feel your lower back muscles tight from a cramped nights rest. You shift your left leg off of the bed and sit up for the first time in the morning. "Time to make the donuts, and Dolly, where's my coffee?" you mumble.

The new nightlight in the bathroom illuminates a path for you to follow. You made sure to plug it in last night because you didn't want a repeat of last weeks adventure. Pitch black, you put your feet on the floor, put the right foot in front of, THUD. That's when you tripped over your yellow labrador, Rachel, hitting your head on the cedar chest at the foot of the bed. That was fun.

Today would be different. Be prepared. That's your new mantra. I am a boy scout. I am a boy scout. I am a boy scout! I am prepared!

After a brisk luke-warm shower, you take a look in the mirror, comb your hair, shave, and brush your teeth. "Now that's what I'm talkin' 'bout."

It's now 5:08 a.m. with time to spare for a quick bite to eat and some of that Dolly Parton coffee she's been singing about. The Keurig is primed and ready to pour a delicious cup of whatever was on sale at the supermarket. Your travel mug was big enough to get two cups out of the single serving packet. Frugal is your middle name!

By 5:30, you've let Rachel outside to do her business, and you're now ahead of the carefully planned schedule you've mapped out to make it to work on time. Leaving the house by 6:00 a.m., you should be able to beat traffic to the office – a mere 30 miles away by 8:00 a.m. Shifting your schedule to these new earlier hours are a great way to be more productive, and get the big boss to really take notice!

5:45 you get into your car, back out of the garage, signal for the door to close, and smile. You're on your way to the office with plenty of time to spare. The surface streets are nearly empty this time of day and you smile to yourself, "Why doesn't everybody get up and get going early. This is a breeze."

About three blocks to the freeway entrance to the 405-northbound, a mirage of hybrids with blinkers blinking in unison like a string of Christmas lights are all signaling for the same thing: freeway freedom. There must be some mistake. Where did all of these cars suddenly come from? They can't all be headed in the same direction with me? I'm prepared! I'm ahead of schedule!

By now you recognize the traffic lights are perfectly timed allowing 4, maybe 5 cars through per cycle. You've still got at least another dozen in front of you before you'll get to the onramp. Looking at the dashboard clock its now 6:12 a.m. and nearly 30 minutes have passed since you left your house, which was less than five miles from here.

A couple more changes in the traffic lights later, you're finally up to the onramp and glad you'll finally be able to make up some "lost time" you spent waiting to get on the freeway.

It's now 6:37 a.m. and you're 19 miles to the office. There's still plenty of time to make it to work – over an hour and twenty minutes. The local morning radio personality on K-Earth 101 is giving the traffic report, which seems laughable since you're cruising along the 405-northbound at 57 mph.

You turn up the volume when Sammy Hagar's "*I Can't Drive 55*" comes on, only to look up and see a see of bright red ahead. The brakes. Hit the brakes! Slow down! Sammy Hagar should be so lucky, driving 55 mph on the 405 at this time of day. The traffic comes to a complete stop. You try to peer off to the left to see if there's any indication of an accident or bodies or police or fire trucks or any logical reason why you'd come to a complete stop on a freeway meant for rapid travel at accelerated speeds. None. You've stopped at 6:43 a.m.

By 6:46 you start moving. Picking up the pace, actually. Cruising right along now at a speedy 14 mph. At one point you even get excited because you're going 37 mph. That lasts for about a quarter mile before the sea of red brakes illuminates the morning sunrise off in the east. 17 miles until you're at the office.

By 7:23 a.m. you've moved along the freeway not much faster than a salted slug, yet you persevere. "It's just 6 more miles... I can do this.. I can do this... I've got 8:00 beat by a mile!" Your office just relocated to a new business park off of Santa Monica Boulevard. Once you get off the freeway, you know it'll be a snap to get to the parking garage and make it to your cubical on time.

You imagine everyone stuck in this nightmare with you this early Monday morning must be as impatient as you. Turning to the car on your right, a young lady with dark brown hair is busy chatting on her cell phone – and texting? She's texting!? She's talking into the phone AND texting! She navigates the steering wheel with her left knee and continues to sit patiently for the other cars to move.

To your left, an older gentleman is busy reading the paper! He's also got an electric razor and he's shaving! He doesn't seemed phased by the lack of movement, either. Business as usual for that businessman. You scan other vehicles and find a college age young man eating a bowl of cereal. Another driver is busy putting on her mascara in the rearview mirror.

This is insanity!

It's time to exit onto Santa Monica and get to the office. It's now 7:48 a.m. and you'll nearly be there on time if everyone does what they're supposed to and gets out of your way. "C'mon people! We've got places to be! Move it like you mean it!" You speed towards the office before being rerouted in another direction because of a new construction project the city just started this morning.

Finally, at 8:27 a.m. you make it to the parking garage, race to the office with sweat dripping down the back of your now wrinkled shirt, hoping to make it to your desk before anyone realizes you're nearly a half hour late for the first day of your early shift to change the world.

"Nice you could make it today, Dave. Might want to get an earlier start tomorrow to join the rest of us who managed to make it here on time."

You nod at your boss with a sheepish smile and do your best to get through the day.

There's always tomorrow's adventures on the 405. Oh Lord, not again…

FORTUITOUS FABLE:

The truth is, I love being a follower. If you want something done, give me a checklist and I'll get it checked off. Need expert notes for the big meeting today? I'll take the most detailed notes you'd hope to review. Give me an idea, and a little freedom, and I'll run with it to create an amazing marketing plan. I turn good ideas into great results. Give me your products and I'll sell the hell out of it and go 200% above goal – every month. It's all about the direction from the top. The leaders you work for and who serve you in return. The people who make you say "Oh Hell Yeah" I'll go on that journey with you.

For the record, I prefer being a follower of a GREAT leader.

I've been continually employed since my first paper route at nine years old delivering the Statesman Journal in Salem, Oregon to fifty-three houses, seven days a week. I did this for six years. Every job I've had since was referred to me. Here's the list:

- Paper Route. Thanks Dad. He hated the paperboy we had, and at 9 years old he asked me, "How'd ya like to make some extra money each month." I had no clue, apart that I knew it would pay more than an allowance.

- Cookie Baker, Server and Toilet Scrubber. Dunkin Donuts. Thanks Derek from Architecture Club. Derek worked at DD and I liked donuts. I'd get a free dozen donuts once a week. Life was a chocolate cream filled dream for 5 months.
- Assistant Manager. First Run Video. When people actually rented VCR's and movies. The owner, Bob Netko, told my friend, "Have Garrett come in and see me..." I liked movies, and I got paid to watch movies while helping customers!
- Salesperson/Warehouse Dude/Accounting Clerk. Two weeks out of high school, I was in Glendale, AZ attending a trade school for architecture. The school's job placement office referred me to this catalog showroom. I started in sales, moved to the gun & camera warehouse to organize it after a remodel, and finally worked in the cash office – all in 10 months.
- Secretary. State of Oregon. Returning home after school in '86, my Dad came

to my aid once again. "Do you want a temp job for the summer?" He was the Director of Human Resources and had connections. I love connections. I started with the Oregon Housing Agency and within 6 months had a permanent job as an administrative assistant with the Oregon State Parks Department. It gave me a "regular" job status, which was good enough to qualify for a car loan for my then-dream car – a brand new 1987 light blue Toyota Celica GT with pop up headlights and a digital dashboard!

- Operator. I moved back to Phoenix in '89 to attend Arizona State and finish up a business degree. I heard about a new job on the local radio station, and drove directly to the building.
- Consultant/Manager. Lured by my friend Jill, I was encouraged to apply for a new department the local phone company was opening. The Home Office Consulting Center (the HOCC as we'd call it) became my first real professional success measured solely by my paychecks. I made great bank!
- Vice-President of Sales. Transportation industry. Referred by a manager I

worked with from my days as an operator, I started in one role, and fourteen years later, it morphed into something entirely different. I'll be the first to say I'm grateful for the opportunities and the big money I made early on. But when they turned the spotlight off, I hung around far too long when I should have been auditioning for my next starring role.

Throughout my careers there were leaders I endured featuring complete morons, people who were blatantly unethical, unprofessional, criminal, spineless, fear mongering, hate spewing, evil doers who were gleeful seeing others miserable. For the record, they officially sucked.

Everytime I would see them coming down the hall, or their extension light up on my phone or an email with their name, my inside voice would always scream, "Oh please Lord, not again." They legitimately created in me PTSD at different times in my life. I hope they never have to work for someone who leaves such negative lasting effects. They make life miserable.

Luckily, in each of these roles, there were also "Oh Hell Yeah" leaders who inspired, motivated, cheered and led their departments to success. I loved working for these people and still enjoy knowing them as we have taken different professional journeys. These are people who made me scream aloud with glee, "Oh hell yeah! You're why I'm here today! Let's go change the world!"

Best selling children's book author, Sheri Fink, shared her "Hell Yes" concept with an audience of writers at the Southern California Writer Association (SCWA) on a bright Saturday morning in 2016. Her enthusiasm to her readers and her vibrant brand are a major "Hell Yes" and I am inspired by her daily.

It makes perfect sense to figure out what makes you happy and make it your "Hell Yes." Do it NOW!

THE ISM TO REMEMBER:
If you spend your time saying, "Oh Hell no...!" It's time for you to go, go, go!

BLOND JESUS-ISM #5:
Oh Hell Yeah

BLOND JESUS-ISM #6

*"You're Stuck With Me"
Isn't Always Forever*

THE ISM OF 6:
Loving someone and being in love, are not the same thing.

PALPABLE PARABLE:
You don't know what "getting divorced" means, but it didn't sound good when you were over at Timmy's earlier playing Nintendo. You asked him if he had to move away and if you'd still be friends. He shook his head giving an "I dunno" look before shooting a dozen more villains in the latest Avengers game. Once you blasted all the bad guys and ate your Lunchable's Dirt Cake snack, you raced home to tell your mom.

"Mommmm! Timmy says his parents are getting divorced!" you pant breathlessly racing in the front door with a sense of pride in knowing something before she does.

"Oh now Johnny," your mother scolds, "nobody likes a tattle tale. Now go to your room and start on your homework. You know how your teacher... She'd be a whole lot easier on you if you'd turn in your homework when she asks..."

You race off to your room to turn on your computer and turn on Netflix. You think to yourself, "Why didn't mom like it when I told her about Timmy's parents? Why did she call me a tattle tale?"

Besides, how old were you when you first heard this? 5, 6, maybe 7? Now that you're nearly 10, you keep hearing it, but don't really know what it means. What's so bad about talking about people anyway? Everyone does it.

The fascination in secrets and gossip has been and will probably always be in all societies. Tonight it's also front and center in your living room at 4:00 when TMZ comes on followed by Entertainment Tonight. Those people in Hollywood are so fascinating! I wonder if they put their pants on one leg at a time or two?

Down the hallway, you hear your mom pick up the phone calling Timmy's mother, "Oh Becky, I just heard the horrible news... Tell me all about it. Uh-huh.... You don't say. That good for nothin'... Why! I never! You poor dear... And then what happened?"

An hour later your father comes home. Your mom can't wait to blab the news either. "Frank, I talked to Becky today. She and Bobby are getting divorced. Apparently Bobby's been dipping the ink the in the company well once too often, with THAT new girl in accounting, what's her name... Kimberly? And..."

Your father, who happens to work with and is best friends with Bobby, isn't aware of the alleged affair. He's known Bobby since college and never thought of his friend as a cheating kind of guy. It bothers your dad so much, he barely touches your mom's famous tri-tip roast and mashed potatoes with homemade gravy. That night, Frank would toss and turn, the information weighing heavy on both his head and his heart.

"Why me? Why now? Why Bobby?" he mumbles in his sleep. Your mom sleeps soundly through the chatter.

In the morning, Frank and Bobby are scheduled to make the biggest advertising pitch of their career to a company who is known for their "traditional family values." How was he going to make it through the presentation after hearing his friend is supposedly a lying, cheating, scumbag? What was he to think?

Meeting early at the clients' offices before the big presentation, Frank confronts Bobby. In a hushed, but stern voice, Frank says, "Bobby! How could you? Right before our big presentation, you go and mess around with *that* Kimberly from accounting? The morality clause in our contract forbids us from doing anything they don't like –and I don't think they are going to like this!"

Bobby, a natural born smooth talker assures Frank, "Listen buddy, you don't know the whole story. We can talk about this later. We don't have time for this now, we have to go in and get this account. I've got a new Mercedes waiting for me at the dealership with the money we'll make on this one! I'll smooth things over with Becky, don't you worry about a thing, Frank."

The client is impressed with the wholesome approach of two fine young family men like Frank and Bobby. They enjoy the stories each share about their children, their wives, how they met, and, of course, their pitch to help them increase sales of their family values widget over the next year.

They land the account. Bobby gets his Mercedes. Becky gets a diamond necklace and all is swept under the carpet. Until Kimberly tells Bobby one day she's pregnant and wants to keep the baby. When Bobby demands Kimberly have an abortion, she causes a major scene in the office. Human Resources is called. Emotions run high. Voices escalate. Lawyers are eventually brought in. Kimberly is encouraged to take a paid leave of absence, until the baby is born and then, well maybe she'd be happier staying at home with the nugget. Bobby is encouraged to find happiness elsewhere. Becky gets the Mercedes, keeps the diamond necklace, and the house.

Bobby moves in with his friend Dan from college, also recently divorced. Between the two of them, they manage enough for a basic DirecTV package and a 36" flat screen which sits on a couple of milk crates.

If only you hadn't told your mom what Timmy had told you that day...

FORTUITOUS FABLE:

I remember growing up watching reruns of Leave it to Beaver on WTBS from Atlanta while folding newspapers at 5:00 a.m. every day. Ward & June always seemed to be so happy and content. Wally and The Beaver would get into mischief and June would remind the boys, "Wait till your father gets home" while looking magnificent in an nice crisply ironed dress and wearing a pearl necklace. How simple life must have been in the 60's if you were white and upper middle class.

Today, a couple generations later, there continue to be plenty of families reminding us that being part of a family is the most important thing in the world. We watched Alex Keaton on *Family Ties* in the 80's to the cast of Modern Family with different combinations of what we now call family – everyone had someone. Your worth in the world is demonstrated nightly on television by your ability to find someone to build a life with.

Granted there are exceptions.

Friends taught us if you' live in a rent controlled apartment in New York, you only knew white people and your first world struggle is determining if you want to date Monica or Phoebe or Ross or Joey or Chandler or Rachel. It's all quite simple. Well, unless your Ross and Rachel – and then nothing is ever simple. However, I think they brought most of that upon themselves.

Growing up I never really thought about getting married or having a family of my own. I think I just liked being by myself, not really having to answer to anyone else in the world. If I wanted to eat ice cream out of the container, I would. If I wanted to watch WWE Monday Night Raw and eat pizza, I would. If I wanted to stay up until 10:30 p.m. on a work night, I would do that too. Doing what I wanted, when I wanted was really cool with me. Thinking about the drama of dating really didn't interest me that much.

Until I hit my mid-20's. Then it hit me hard. "I'm never going to find anyone! I'll never meet someone who loves me! Am I un-loveable? What's my problem? Everyone else has a boyfriend/girlfriend or, gulp, they're getting married! I should be doing this too! There must be some Kardashians I need to be keeping up with somewhere! Where are they –

oh I'm so far behind the curve, I'll never catch up!"

That's not the best reason to ever get involved in a relationship, yet it was the barometer of where I was at in my life. I had to find someone and settle down! My clock was ticking! I'd be 30 in 4 years and, gasp, if you're single by the time you're 30 – you might as well have one foot in the grave. You're done. Turn the lights out! Go home. Alone!

By this point, I knew I was gay and dating hot chicks probably wasn't in my future. For the record – I love hot chicks. I dig the ladies! Most of my best friends are women. You rock! But I'm gay, and, well, I'm a much better lunch date for an hour of your time to gab over a low-calorie salad and ice water with a slice or two of lemon.

My dating life wasn't very successful. Each attempt started off great – meet at a bar, through friends, at a party – wherever – long before Grindr hookup apps existed. There was a time, believe it or not, you actually met and talked with the person you were interested in – in real time. Hella concept. Each started out the same – hot and heavy, seeing each other every night for the first week. By the second or third week, it would be a few times a week. At the end of the first month, maybe you were seeing one another on the weekends and maybe talking on the phone once during the week to check in.

If that sounds familiar, you were probably dating me!

I'm not sure what I was doing right or wrong – apart from being enthusiastic about meeting someone I *thought* I liked. Maybe the outpouring of affection with gifts or food or restaurants or whatever was too much? You know, all of the things I hated when someone would try to do that for me – I was doing the exact same thing.   I'll do the chasing around here, thankyouverymuch.

I spent a lot of my time being single worrying I would never meet someone who could ever possibly love me. Ever. That's a long time. Ever.

How and why did I get so insecure? I swear I got enough hugs growing up. And gosh darn it, people liked me.

My first "real" relationship left me emotionally crushed. It lasted around 2 years. Remember the old joke, "How long have you been married?" And the punch line, "We've been happily married 11 years, married for 26..." In my desperation to put myself into a relationship, my first "long-term" attempt, which should have been a casual date for a week, endured because we both were scared we would never find anyone ever again.

That, for the record, is a horrible reason to be in a relationship.

A couple years passed without any real dates or faux-relationships to speak of. Until one night I was at Roscoe's on 7th in Phoenix. I was there to meet friends who never showed up. Going to a bar alone wasn't really my thing, so while I waited, I caught a glimpse of this cute guy at the end of the bar. He was there with friends.

As I choose to re-tell the story now, I finally managed the courage to hang out over by the pool tables – closer to where he was sitting. His friend gave him a nudge off of his chair and pushed him in my direction.

He walked up to me and smiled.

I asked him, "Do you have a boyfriend?"

He replied, "No."

I said, "Do you want one?"

He smiled back and said, "Yes."

And the rest, shall we say, is history.

We were together for 12 years. We laughed a lot. We loved a lot. We bought cars together. We built a custom home together. We became puppy parents together. We took vacations together. We shared our families and events together. We played video games together. We watched movies together. We had lots of fun.

Early in our relationship when we decided we wanted to make things more official, we even signed pieces of paper to each other reading, "You are stuck with me," signed our names and gave each other the paper to keep in our wallets. It was silly, but a symbol of our commitment.

I was pretty much a functioning wreck during the majority of our time together for one reason or another. I give him all of the credit for putting up with me, tolerating my erratic behavior, and still choosing to love me despite all of the horrible things I'd say and do. At the end of the day, the "being together" part of our relationship ran its course and it was time to set him free or risk completely blowing up whatever good was left between us. That was the hardest thing I'd ever done. I don't like to be the bad guy for myself.

It's now been 4 years since we've split up. The first few weeks were weird. I think people have this concept when you breakup, you should never want to speak to that person ever again. Except, we still liked each other as people, but the relationship just didn't work. It feels so Ben & Jen or Chris & Gwyneth. Well, we do live in Southern California.

After the breakup, he moved to an apartment a few miles away for the first year. When the bungalow in the front had a vacancy, he moved "home" the following spring. Living 10' away, we still text each all the time. He comes over to the shared laundry room and plays with the dogs during the spin cycle.. They go nuts when "papa" is here on Thursdays. He is family to me. He always will be. Yet, he has his life now, and I have mine. There is real love, and respect, between us. I am grateful.

THE ISM TO REMEMBER:
Loving someone and being in love are not the same thing.

BLOND JESUS-ISM #6:
"You're Stuck With Me" Isn't Always Forever

BLOND JESUS-ISM #7

*Feed Your Spirit With Love and
It Will Love You Back*

THE ISM OF 7:
Whatever you're trying to escape from will eventually find you. Deal with it and move on with your life.

PALPABLE PARABLE:
Growing up in the 60's & 70's you only watched tv shows on 4 channels; ABC, CBS, NBC and PBS. Maybe another one or two if you grew up in a big city. You turned the channels of the tv by getting up off of the plastic covered sofa, walking over to the console and actually turning the knob. Hopefully the channel change didn't screw up the antenna on the roof,

or you may have been forced to wear tin foil on your head and stand next to the set trying to get better reception while your family gathered to watch Room 222 or the Mod Squad. They're real shows people, you can look 'em up. Remote controls didn't exist until the late 70's. Again, you can look this up; this is how people lived "back in the day." Fo realz.

On a lot of shows, it was common to see people smoking cigarettes and having a martini during lunch, dinner, after making love, or even driving to the grocery store to get more diapers for the kids who you'd protect with an arm across the chest should you be forced to come to a sudden stop. Despite wars and conflict, we still had our parent's arm across our chest as we stood in the front seat waving our arms out the window at the neighbors. There were no real consequences. Everyone lived happy lives, in happy neighborhoods, in happy homes, with perfect jobs, perfect spouses, perfect children, and delicious delightful Swanson TV dinners. The Salisbury Steak was always a personal favorite.

Eventually, for some crazy reason smoking finally got banned from TV shows and advertising. Something about it being dangerous for your health. Luckily, people could still find solace in a whisky or bourbon on late night TV. The legendary Larry Hagman's *JR* on *Dallas* would always be pouring a drink to seal a deal, celebrate a conquest, or just plain stew and complain to his momma, *Miss Ellie* about someone tryin' to do him wrong. Each episode featured someone drinking, or perpetually drunk and getting into mischief. Apparently it's what all the cool kids at Southfork did. Especially *JR's* long suffering wife, *Sue Ellen*. How much could a beauty queen take before she'd hit the bottle again? About three episodes.

By the late 80's, in real life, Larry was told he had to get a liver transplant from all his years of hard drinking. That's also the same time the Dallas set replaced liquor with apple juice and ginger ale, and fewer scenes focused on dealing with life's challenges by celebrating with a bottle. Finally, we could get back to good old fashioned back stabbing, secret alliances and returning from the dead - all because of a season long bad dream!

Being drunk and disorderly ran its course on most television shows – watching a bunch of drunks just wasn't fun anymore. At least not on scripted tv. Sporting events are entirely different. Every major, minor, and wannabe team in virtually every sport wants a beer sponsorship. Miller's, Coors, Budweiser, Corona, Dos Equis, even Pabst Blue Ribbon line up to court teams, events and anything remotely connected to sport. Including poker.

Some of the most memorable commercials for major sporting events come from beer. Remember the three frogs from the Superbowl a few years back? Bud-Wise-Er. Or, horses pulling a sleigh full of beer through the snow. Cold beer delivered to you in the snow when you're already freezing. There's some logic for you.

A more recent favorite focused on a golden retriever puppy falling in love with a Clydesdale. How they met remains a mystery. Said puppy keeps escaping to the neighbors' farm to see his true love. Picture this: the good looking, yet "annoyed" male neighbor returns the good looking puppy to the good looking female neighbor. A hint of flirting takes place between the humans. Apparently nobody in this farming community is married. The puppy is finally recaptured "once and for all" by his owner and is seen being driven home in the cleanest car ever to drive down a dusty country road – only to be stopped by the Clydesdale and the Clydesdale's posse who surround the car on this dust-free dirt road. How they escaped the barn and raced down the road to find the car… Well, the next thing we see the puppy is running free down the road, followed by the team of Clydesdales, presumably back to the pretty lady's farm. The plot lines are so rich with opportunity for sequels you forget you're being sold a love story about Budweiser beer. Yeah, they have their logo appear the entire commercial and a nice brand message at the end. Isn't that sweet? Who need's another Bud?

In the lives of most adults it's probably safe to say many have had a drink or two. Or thirteen or fourteen. Or lost count and blacked out. The bitter biting grasp of that first chug of beer. Can you ever forget how it tasted as it bubbled on your tongue and coarsely went down your throat? The ensuing belch worthy of a blue ribbon from said Pabst. Or the sip of the sugary fruity-tootie with an umbrella and a cherry on top that wasn't quite right. It's the first swig that both grosses you out and brings you back in. Trusting your friends that if you chug it, you'll feel better, loosen up, and *finally* have a good time.

Now it's 2:00 a.m. when everyone else at the bar has put on a thick layer of beer goggles and found someone *gorgeous* to take home – some even with their spouse! How are you going to get home? Where's your phone? Your friends left you behind! Can you blame them? After your rousing off-key rendition of "*She Bangs*" by Ricky Martin during the karaoke contest, followed by your insistence to debate the best free-throw shooter in NBA history with a table of grandmothers in from DuBuque, the fun just kept on getting funner. Eventually you passed out in the bathroom, after barfing your guts into oblivion into a questionably clean toilet.

You'd tell yourself the next day, "Dry heaves are not how I want to get six-pack abs." You passed 6-pack abs for a couple of 2-litres years ago. Look in the mirror. Who are you kidding?

Thankfully, your friends captured these Kodak moments and posted everything to Facebook and Twitter. Including the video of you hitting on your best friend's wife. That was cute.

You chalk it up to having some fun. You're young. You're old. You're stressed. You're cold. You're lonely. You're in love. You're celebrating your new job. You're crying over getting fired – again.   Your friends are in town. Your friends left town. It's the big game. It's happy hour with the gang. It's Saturday night. You're letting off some steam.

Except the steam starts getting let off more often than just Saturday nights at the sports bar down the road.

You tell yourself, "This going out and getting drunk all the time is really getting out of hand. I need to get my act together. I'll just stop at the liquor store on the way home and pick up a 12 pack so I can unwind once I get back to the house. After all, it would be easier, and cheaper, just to stay home during the week – save's money on the babysitter, and, well, after the last parent teacher conference, I'm supposed to help little Susie with her homework; and I've got that quarterly report on the widgets to finish while pretending to listen to what my partner wants to complain about. If I'm lucky, I might stay up late for some Fallon on The Tonight Show. I probably should get 2-12 packs today so I can just come straight home tomorrow and get busy helping my family."

FORTUITOUS FABLE:

From my Facebook post January 22, 2016.

Happy Birthday to me. Today marks my 3rd Birthday of getting sober. Last year's post on Facebook got tons of PM's of your own struggles and successes, and for a moment I wasn't going to make a big deal this year. Why? Lots of friends are posting milestones of 5, 7, 9, 10, 15, 23 years of being clean. So what will a measly 3 and banter by me really do for anyone, or myself?

Perspective. Today as I start a fresh new year, it's important to remember how I used to deal with things and how I live life today.

Last year was filled with skyscraper highs and Grand Canyon lows. The old me used to celebrate every high point with drinks, and any disappointment with more drinks. It was easy to rationalize drinking was fun and festive, or numbing and escaping. Last year's roller coaster provided plenty of reasons to get bombed!

I've previously shared the sole reason I got sober: vanity. I woke up one day and finally saw my bloated body standing in the mirror. I was 50 pounds heavier, and 235 at my worst. There are few pictures of me found between 2000-2012 – mainly because I couldn't stand the sight of how I looked. Delete, delete, delete! Yes, I freely admit the main reason I stopped drinking was to look good. The benefits – emotional, physical and spiritual were just additional perks I'd enjoy later.

After last years 2nd birthday, momentum with the fun creative projects left me excited like no other time in my life. The highest of the highs! At the same time behind the scenes, the old routine changed how the game was played, which left me financially devastated and humbled to the core.

All were great reasons in the past to have "just one."

I knew "just one" would lead to "oh, I can have just one more" and then the old routine would kick in. Thankfully, the thought of the taste alcohol was enough to keep me from taking a sip. Blech! But there were multiple occasions of dark thoughts crossing my mind about my life's events. At the grocery store, I'd walk by the liquor isle and wonder if I should take a slower stroll. Then holidays were here, which are always the hardest, for a variety of reasons – including evenings getting dark earlier. If you need a list of reasons to feel sorry for yourself – let me know, mine's a mile long and I'll gladly share with you. I want more sunshine! It's dark too early! Time for a drink! That used to work for me.

However, at the end of the day now I remember how much I hate the taste of alcohol, until after that first drink or until I'd get too blitzed to care. I remember now how groggy I'd feel the next morning after getting a lousy night's sleep from being drunk and passing out, again. I remember people in my life I easily discarded because drinking was more important to me than being loved and accepted.

Interestingly, last Sunday I ran into a friend who leaned in as if to hear a classified top secret and whispered, "Have you cheated in the last 3 years? You know, even one drink..." I replied a bit shocked at his question, "Nope. Not a one."

Today, I clearly know drinking doesn't serve my higher purpose, so I focus on the bigger picture. That last line was so easy to type and it sounds so incredibly sanctimonious. Sorry.

This year was a return to basics. I prayed, meditated and wrote in my journals. I cried, screamed and felt sorry for myself so often I lost count. The Whoa-Ez-Me Trail of Tears regularly passed my front door. I'm not proud of sharing with you the "yuck factor" but this was my reality in 2015.

Now each morning before I get out of bed I begin saying "Thank you" to God for giving me a great new day. I say it over and over and over in my head and aloud as the puppies wake up and begin shaking their heads like mini alarm clocks. I smile with a grateful heart that I've got a roof over my head, healthy and delicious food to eat, a fun car to drive, good friends who genuinely care about me, creative projects which are gaining successful momentum, and that I'm awake with clear thoughts in my head, and sober.

Once my feet hit the floor and before turning on the computer, I open a special notebook and write out my "God and Angels list." On one side of the paper I jot down 3 things I have to do today. On the other side, I write down everything else in life weighing on me and begin with "God, I am asking for your help now..." and write until I can't think of anything else. Then I put the notebook away and begin my day. Every day. At night before I drift to sleep, I end my final waking thoughts by saying "Thank you" over and over.

You might think that's silly. That's okay. I'm not looking for your approval or validation. It's what I do. This is what works for me now.

FYI: I've never been to a 12-step meeting. I haven't gone to rehab. I haven't done a lot of things others have done to get sober. Some days are easier than others. Some days, frankly suck. But I know, for me, being sober is so much better than the alternative. I spent too many wasted years *being wasted*. I've got things I am doing now I never thought possible because I finally said, "Enough is enough."

If you're wondering if you can do it, YES YOU CAN! Find your reason to get sober and do it NOW. Write it down. Keep it in front of your eyes at all times. Find the help that works for *you*. Yes, it totally sucks having to deal with life sometimes. Other days, reality is pretty awesome now. But when the urge is strong, find something to distract you for a hot minute and stay your course! If you are struggling today, send me an email if you need to chat with someone. I'll do my best to be an ear for you. And remember, if I can do it, you can too.

Happy Birthday to me. And many, many more.

THE ISM TO REMEMBER:
Whatever you're trying to escape from will eventually find you. Deal with it and move on with your life.

BLOND JESUS-ISM #7:
Feed Your Spirit With Love and It Will Love You Back

BLOND JESUS-ISM #8

Hanging Out at the Suckerberg's Cliff of Lemmings

THE ISM OF 8:
If you're ready to jump every time someone posts a meme... here, read mine, "Don't jump!"

PALPABLE PARABLE:
Remember when you were 6 and started making friends at school outside of the carefully supervised confines of your living room and the watchful eyes of your parents? At first, it's scary walking into the classroom for the first time, with your hair combed neatly, your new sneakers tied tightly, and the fancy new outfit coordinated perfectly.

"My little Johnny! He can't live without meeeeeeeeeeeee!" your mother screams down the hallway as the Principal Pinecone and a grief counselor drag her by her arms towards the exit.

Principal Pinecone, "Let me assure you that Johnny, along with the other 31 munchkins, will be in expert hands with Mrs. Hippie's first grade class at Morningside Elementary School. Now please, Mrs. Crocker, you must regain your composure! He's in one of the best classrooms and with one of our most popular teachers! He will be just fine. Now, please... don't you have some cookies to bake? Come back at 2:30 and you can pick him up. Bring chocolate chip."

Mascara-stained tears smear her otherwise beautiful face. Your mom slowly returns to the family station wagon, a pale lemon yellow Buick, gets in and waits. Ten minutes later, she wrings her hangs one more time, checking her face in the rearview mirror while wiping her eyes with a tissue. "Surely the school nurse will race out at any moment and confirm what I've known all along –Johnny cannot live without me by his side!"

Nope. Impossible.

By this time, you've forgotten what your mom looks like and what all the fuss was about just a few short moments ago. You're sitting next to your new friends Billy and Alison, twins. Their mother, Amanda, runs a high profile advertising firm in Los Angeles and has already encouraged these youngsters to think outside those baked up box of rules your parents instilled with you since you were christened with the nickname Johnny Cakes.

Your attention span is short, so when Mrs. Hippie tells the class to go outside and play for 15 minutes, you shake with excitement. You line up single file and wait for your teacher to blow the whistle. Then, and only then, can you make a mad dash to the playground.

The whistle blows and a hurricane of dust bunnies swirl past the door and clamor for the fresh air. The freedom to run amok, amok, amok is lost on you as Billy and Allison wave you over to the monkey bars.

"C'mon, Johnny, you gotta do the monkey bars! Billy and I are!" Allison says with authority.

Your parents always told you that you needed to be 8 before you got on the monkey bars and kids your age were too small. It was dangerous.

"Nah, that's ok... my mom said I'm too young..."

"You're still a baby. Are you wearing a diaper? I bet you pooped your pants!" Billy teases.

"I'm not a baby! I'm going to get into trouble if I do it."

"Who's going to tell? Yeah, you're a baby. A big baby tattle tale. Johnny's a baby! Johnny's a baby! No wonder your mom was crying, she didn't want to leave her baby all by himself..." Allison laughes.

"I'm not a baby!"

"Prove it," Billy demands and then scales across the bars without much fanfare. He's had practice shows off for Johnny, the novice.

"I've never been on the monkey bars... I..."

"Cuz Johnny's a baby! Johnny's a baby!" they chime in unison.

Their chants are louder and someone might hear. The rest of the school may find out they're right – you're a baby. A scared-y cat! You don't want the other kids in the class to think you're a baby. Plus your new best friends already think you're a baby. There's only one thing left to do lest you suffer an eternal humiliation of being proven a baby – cross those monkey bars!

Nervous you'll get in trouble if your mom finds out, you make your way to the bars. You take ahold of the pole, and raise yourself up the 3 steps up to the top position. You take turns wiping your sweaty hands on your denim jeans copying what you saw Billy and Allison do. In your gut, you know you shouldn't being up here, nearly 2' off the ground and without your parents nearby, but you aren't a baby! You are going to show them!

You reach up and grab the top rung with your right hand with enough strength to juice a hard lemon. Then your left hand grabs ahold of the top rung.

"Go ahead, or are you a big baby? Baby! Baby! Baby!"

You push off with both feet and are hanging there not sure what to do next. The pull on your hands is strong, even if you only weigh 53 lbs. You reach out for the second rung with your right hand and make contact. You grab onto this as tightly as you can. Then you reach with your left hand and.... You fall and land on your left arm.

This hurts more than anything you've ever felt before. It hurts so much that you begin crying uncontrollably. Hearing your screaming, Mrs. Hippie races over, "What is going on? You children shouldn't be up on these!"

Billy and Allison scurry away. You're left a blubbering snot-faced mess. Mrs. Hippie calls for assistance from another teacher and help get you to the office. The school nurse takes over and begins to assess the damage.

"Does it hurt when I touch your arm h...." Nurse Nancy asks. But before gets out the last word, you scream loud enough that Principal Pinecone pops his head in to see what's going on.

"Oh no..." he says under his breath, "it's barely the first day of school and we've already got a casualty..."

Nurse Nancy is careful not to move your arm further. She gets an ice pack out of the freezer in the teacher's lounge and puts it on to help keep the swelling down. "Please call Johnny's mother and have her come get him. He's going to need to see a doctor and get this arm x-rayed."

Midway through mixing ingredients for her award-winning blue ribbon cookies, the phone rings. Your mom sets her sugar-filled measuring cup down on the counter, wipes her hands on her red-checkerboard apron, and answers, "Hello. This is Betty..."

"Mrs. Crocker, it's Principal Pinecone, I'm afraid we have some bad news... Little Johnny fell and hurt his arm during recess. We need you to come pick him up and take him to the doctor. He may have broken his arm."

The olive green phone is already dangling by its curly cord, as your mom is in the car and half way down the street as the Principal continues talking...

Your arm hurts really bad and you think you're going to die, but when you see your Mom race through the doors to the nurses office, you know real help is on the way. After a few loud words between your mom and the Principal, she comes into the room and gives you a big kiss on the forehead. It's at this point you know you're going to be ok.

"Oh Johnny! I knew I should never have left you alone!" she moans. "Mama's going to make it all better. We're going to see the Dr. Welby now." She helps you up and carefully braces your arm with your favorite Batman blanket she managed to remember between dropping the phone and magically reappearing at school.

Once the x-rays come back to confirm the suspicions, your arm is set into a cast. Not bad for the first half of the first day of school. You get through the tears and emotions of this traumatic event. On the way home, you're so relieved your mom has saved you and is taking you home. You wonder if she'll give you 2 cookies or 3 because of all you've gone through today.

You poor... baby...

Instead, your mom lovingly turns to you and says, "Johnny, I'm so glad you're alright and going to be better. But now I need to know what happened today... You need to tell me everything that happened, and if you leave anything out, mommy's going to be very upset. Start talking."

Shocked, and no mention of cookies, you blurt, "Mom, they were calling me a baby! And I didn't poop my pants. They said I was a baby if I didn't cross the monkey bars. I'm not a baby, mommy. I'm not," you begin crying again. The fresh memories of Billy and Allison chiding you at recess this morning rings loud in your ears.

"You poor dear... My poor Johnny... No, you're not a baby, Johnny, you're a sucker! How many times have your father and I told you when you are 8 that's when you can play on the monkey bars? HOW MANY TIMES, YOUNG MAN? How old you right now, this very day?"

"Mom, you know I'm 6, we ju..."

"SIX! Is 6 the same as 8? Answer me!"

"Nn....no..."

"Well someone's getting an A in math today. BINGO! You're right. 6 is not 8. And since 6 is not 8, what does that mean? Answer me!"

"But they were calling me baby, and you don't understand."

"Understand what? Your arm is broken. You're in tears. And now, you've missed the rest of the first day of school. Do you know what this means? DO YOU?"

"That you'll bake me cookies when we get home?"

"NO! Your broken arms means you will NOT get cookies when we get home. You are going straight to your room, and you are going to stay there the rest of the day. Wait until your father gets home!"

"But mom, that's not fair!"

"I'll tell you what's not fair, Johnny. People like Billy and Allison getting you to do something you know isn't right by calling you names and making fun of you. That's not fair. Yet you bought into their baloney anyway, didn't you?"

"Yeah, but..."

"But now your arm is broken and in a cast for the next 6 weeks. You listened to people you don't even know about something they, themselves, know nothing about, and you end up with a broken arm. Your brain should be in a cast instead of your arm!"

You both sit in silence for the remainder of the drive. Back at the house, you head off to your room to ponder the meaning of life. You wonder if you'll get dessert tonight after dinner? Mom's made another great cake. Would you be allowed to stay up and watch Modern Family and The Middle? There would be many crucial decisions to be made later today.

One thing's for sure you: know you're going to think twice before listening to your new friends again.

FORTUITOUS FABLE:

In this age of information at your fingertips, you'd think people you know would be a lot more.... I dunno, smart, given the fact you can Google pretty much anything in 3 seconds or less. Yet day after day I'm constantly amazed at how dumb people are. Truly, truly dumb. And these are smart people. Or at least people I'd hoped were smart enough to know better.

I'm reminded of the scene in the 1992 movie, **Death Becomes Her**, where Goldie Hawn (*Helen Sharp*), Bruce Willis (*Ernest Menville*), Meryl Streep (*Madeline Ashton*) and Isabella Rossellini (*Lisle Von Rhuman*) all chase the secret to eternal youth and beauty. If you haven't seen this classic social commentary, this is a must for anyone who enjoys dark comedy with a great message.

The basic premise is Helen and Madeline were friends in college. Madeline goes off to Hollywood and becomes a big star. Left behind, a frumpy Helen meets Ernest and they get engaged. Turns out, Ernest has a big crush on Madeline. Helen tests his love for her by attending one of Madeline's plays. Madeline learns that Ernest is a doctor. She sees opportunity. He sees stars. Helen sees red.

Fast forward several years and we find that Ernest dumped Helen, married Madeline, and settled into an unhappy marriage in Beverly Hills. Madeline's career is fading and not even a boy toy on the side can bring her happiness.

One day, Madeline gets an invitation to a book signing by Helen. She attends and is stunned to see a statuesque Helen welcome her. *"Mad,"* Helen says. *"Hell..."* Madeline replies. Helen's changed, and it does not please Madeline.

Through her plastic surgeon, Madeline stumbles upon Lisle. She makes her way to a castle in the Hollywood hills, meets the gorgeous Lisle, and is promised eternal youth.

Once Madeline gulps the fountain of youth potion, Lisle says cautiously, *"Now a warning."*

To which Madeline replies, *"NOW A WARNING?!"*

That's what it's like many days when I open up Facebook or Twitter and see people's posts about politics and dead celebrities. It's numbing to see people who you've had intelligent conversations with share "news" about a certain political candidate or social issue.

They'll leave an impassioned statement like, "This is why we can't have nice things. It's all So-N-So's fault." If you dare click on the fake news article to see what inane insanity awaits, sometimes the articles are done from a certain political slant. It doesn't matter if it's Republican or Democrat or Independent, they all have the same dummied down rhetoric that gets people all riled up. I get it. People from one side write nonsense about the other to help get more people to think/vote/act/share the same mentality. Great. Love it. Except when the facts are misquoted, worse – made up. Fake news sites be damned!

It's these made up facts that "intelligent" people get on board with so quickly that I find the most disturbing. Seriously, you didn't bother to fact check simple basics like the SOURCE or the article? When people go ballistic and forward articles written by weird sources, isn't that the first clue for lack of authenticity? I mean, when articles aren't being reported from credible news sources like

Huffington Post, CNN, Yahoo or, well, any other mainstream publication, how does jumping on board the looney tune express seem rationale?

The meme craze is equally painful. Candidate A gets some brainiac to write a meme showing the candidate on one side, an ape in a zoo on the other. The caption reads with some smartass comment like, "Raised by Apes. Born To Be Wild. Who knows which is which?" Baiting tactics have sparked a primal chord with society and this is what we react to now. If we see it on the internet, it must be true!

Is it a wonder why, then, we get riled up by the non-news of the news? Is it better to believe the invented story when no other story seems to be riling enough people up? Social media has been a great tool for people to finally have a voice for anything and everything they are passionate about. I love it. It's great. And yet it comes without any training manual, certificate of proficiency or reality check. The battle cry of "Let's show everyone how gullible and dumb we are today" is shouted far too often. By far too many people.

Case in point. Bob Denver. Gary Coleman.

Don Knotts. Bea Arthur. Elvis Presley. They've been dead for YEARS! And this list of dead celebrities goes on. And on. And on. I love when people share horribly tragic news and think they're the first to report it. What purpose does your "reporting" serve? Are we really going to start relying on Facebook friend Mary from Montana for her breaking news of celebrity deaths? No, Mary, we do not expect nor rely upon *you* to break dead celebrity news to us. Ever. So please stop.

Case in point, Mary posts Don Knotts just died, except its 2016. If Mary simply clicked on the article to see it was written in 2006, though shares it like its fresh today... Mary, you look like an idiot. Especially with your comment, "RIP: Too Soon."

Another not-yet-dead Celebrity posting recently showcased Tina Tuner on the cover of Vogue with the headline, *"Tina Tuner Lands Her First Ever Vogue Cover"* and talks about this 73 year old legend... Yay for Tina! Except the post in 2016 references a 2013 article as if it's today's news. Comments of, "Go Tina! You still look great!" Again, nobody read the actual post date to see it happened over 3 years ago. I'm sure Ms. Turner still stuns and looks great, but can you please fact check a friggin' simple thing like the publication date before posting your "breaking news?"

Please, go to sleep comfortably tonight knowing you are NOT our trusted news source – for anything! You no longer have to pretend to be CNN's Headline News correspondent for Facebook. You'll look a lot smarter in the future.

THE ISM TO REMEMBER:
If you're ready to jump every time someone posts a meme... here, read mine, "Don't jump!"

BLOND JESUS-ISM 8:
Winners Aren't Lemmings Jumping Off A Cliff

BLOND JESUS-ISM #9

I'm Going To Rule The World When I Grow Up

THE ISM OF 9:
You can do everything, if you think you can.

PALPABLE PARABLE:
It starts early. Unintentional. New parents bring these fresh little things called *babies* home from the hospital and delude themselves into thinking "we're not going to be like our parents… we're evolved… we're better… we're educated… we're wealthy… we're in the right school district." No matter how many books read during the prior 9 months of joy about how to be the perfect parent, it's not possible.

Its no surprise parents want the best for their kids. "We won't make our kids play sports like I had to when I was growing up!" "No music lessons for this one! I hated my piano teacher growing up – she had bad breath!" "We are going to let little Suzie and Johnny organically become the human beings they were brought into this world to be." Yeah, right. That lasts about 18 seconds until the crying begins. Bathe me! Change me! Feed me! Rock me! All are cries you make to your spouse as you're nerves are frayed after yet another sleepless night with a newborn.

Once your little ones let you sleep through the night, you start thinking about their personalities and what they'll be like as they begin to grow. "Suzie is clearly the smartest child ever in the history of all recorded children, she will be a scientist and get a doctorate in aerospace technology by the time she's 18." "Johnny is so good at writing, he'll grow up to be an English professor at Stanford." No, you're not putting your own expectations or judgments on your kids at all. Not at all. And not at this early age.

Yet, when their teeth come in, their hair grows out, and their bodies develop into young adults, many ideas about the "you should" and "you shouldn't" have become engrained in their heads whether intentionally or not, well meaning or not. And here you are 18 years later, standing wearily at a high school graduation, hoping that your proud bundle of joy, will make something of himself and finally move out of your house so you can run around naked again!

"Good thing Suzie got that scholarship to Princeton... there's no way I could have paid for that!" "Good thing Johnny got into the Community College so he can get his first two years out of the way and hopefully get his GPA up so he can get into a state college down the road."

Funny thing is, by this time, Suzie and Johnny have their own ideas about what they're capable of. It all started with you – and if you didn't fuck it up too badly after your third divorce and a brief stay at that conference (a.k.a. rehab), hopefully they're at a baseline of decent human beings. That's all you can hope for. It's about the same as what your parents gave to you. And what theirs gave to them. The technology and times may have changed, but human behavior keeps on repeating itself.

Suzie gets to Princeton and starts taking classes in molecular biology. She's aced her first set of mid-terms and is ready to become the new Albert Einstein. One weekend, her dorm roommate, Adele, suggests going to see her latest boyfriend, Serge, who is a chef at a local Benihana's. She reasons she could use a break from the around the clock studying, and hanging out with Adele, "Hello - what more could a best friend want?"

Suzie and Adele are seated at a prime table in the center of the restaurant. Serge, the star chef, is putting on a great show. Slicing, dicing, chopping and searing the meal right in front of their eyes! Suzie had never seen something so exciting and fun before! The dinner flies by and on the way home, Suzie asks Adele about Serge's background. "Serge was a dishwasher first. Then he worked his way up, and now he's the main attraction everyone comes to see prepare their meal at Benihana!"

"I'd love to do something so fun for a career!" Suzie would tell Adele. "But my parents would kill me. From the time I was old enough to look through the telescope, it's always been, 'You're our little shooting star, Suzie, and one day you're going to grow up to be a scientist who sends rockets into space!'" Suzie goes on to become a rocket scientist, makes a spaceship load of money, buys a really big house with a really big mortage in a privately gated community, and wonders when she will be happy.

You are so proud of your little Suzie. "She's so successful!" you tell your friends. This is your version of what happy looks like.

Now where's Johnny. Oh yeah, he's back at the Community College, taking classes, getting back on course and doing exactly what he's always been told. He does a fine job with a 3.25 GPA, lives off campus in a 70'st style apartment complex with his high school friend Matt, who's also taking the same classes. After graduating with an AA at the Community College, Johnny attends State University and graduates in 4 years. Johnny applies to several colleges nearby, but ultimately is offered a job teaching back at the same Community College where he attended. Plus, it's right around the corner from home. While he has his own apartment now, he still comes over several nights a week for dinner and helps with the yard work now that you're getting older. Like 56 is old! But you don't refuse the help.

At Johnny's 10-year high school reunion this

year, he ran into his old roommate Matt. "So whatever happened to you, Johnny? Did you get that big professor job at Stanford?"

"No Matt. My parents like having me around. I'm not sure they'd know what to do if I moved away. I've got an apartment nearby. They need me to keep them company."

"Did they get into some accident or get sick?" Matt asks

"Oh no, I just like hanging out with them. They're my best friends." Johnny concedes.

Johnny's life is now set a course for his next 30 years. He's got a steady job and comes home to his 1 bedroom apartment playing Final Fantasy on Xbox after grading papers. He'll never venture far from his Oxford Comma, either. You'll also never be running around the house naked, at least not with Johnny nearby.

FORTUITOUS FABLE:

Lots of stuff has happened to me between the time I was born and when I turned 45ish. While I've said it before, or at least I thought I have, it bears repeating so I can make sure I've said it, "I don't really remember much of my old life." I think it's true the saying about you might not remember what someone said to you, but you'll always remember how they made you feel.   Much of my past is gone. Whether it's intentionally blocking out certain events, being drunk out of my mind and blacking out, or just with time passing and only so much room in the hard drive of my brain, I'm not the world's greatest historian of my life. Maybe I should have started journaling 40 years ago. Would it be the world's least interesting retrospective or todays equivalent to War and Peace? We'll never know, and frankly, I'm not sure I want to know any longer.

There are memories, for sure, from growing up. Some memories make my heart warm and fuzzy, while others created heartache which I dealt with by building walls to protect it from additional damage. I think we're probably all in the same boat, but how we handle the events in our lives, and the people who say things to us —well that's another story.

So many of what I do recall as 'defining moments' came from what people said, how they made me feel, and how I chose to respond and live with these feelings – sometimes for decades.

I'm not sure when I decided that I needed to be the perfect little people pleasing boy, who would grow up into the perfect people pleasing employee, who would be the perfect fill in the blank. It did, however, start early.

Was I afraid of getting into trouble by Mrs. Evans, my second grade teacher at Morningside Elementary School by playing "Six Million Dollar Man" in the wrong part of the hilltop playground with my friends Roger and Stacy (who'd play Jamie Summers a.k.a. The Bionic Woman)? I always wanted to be Steve Austin and marry Jamie Summers.

Was it getting a scolding from my Dad Saturday nights in the YMCA swimming pool for sneaking up on people floating on innertubes tickling their feet?

I thought it was hysterical.

Was it getting yelled at by my Mom for not coming home from the park across the busy street when I said I would? She thought I'd surely been hit by a car. Earlier I'd begged, "Just 30 more minutes, Mom… c'mon!" I was around 6 at the time and had no concept of time or a watch. So there was that.

Getting into minor trouble and the thought of getting into more trouble didn't appeal to me. Much like a dog longing for the love of their ower, I "think" I learned quickly to be a good boy. Sit when I was told to sit. Stay when I was told to stay. And do whatever I needed to do to be the perfect angel.

Was I always the perfect angel? Hardly. Both of my parents can share stories about how I tested their patience. Thankfully, they still loved me even when I was a complete snot – which was often. I'm not sure I could have done the same if I were in their shoes. Well, I know I would never choose to have a Freaky Friday happen.

To the outside world, Garrett tried to be a perfect little angel, never a trouble-maker and always wanted good to win over evil every day.

What I do know is that both of my parents, as best as they could, always encouraged me to grow up and be whatever I wanted to be. By the time I got into my junior and senior years of high school, I had a good run of "ignorance is bliss" – if there was something I wanted to do, I just figured out a way to do it.

From being a professional wrestling photographer with feature articles in the worlds largest pro wrestling publications in 1983, to singing my first song in 2013, "Tell Me Something More." Both achievements happened with a healthy dose of ignorance is bliss. I didn't listen to anyone who'd say, "You can't do that! That doesn't make sense! Who would do that at your age, anyway?" I only focused what the goal was and then took action to make it happen.

When the first wrestling magazine returned my pictures from an amateur photography contest with a type written note, "Your pictures are too professional for this, and therefore we cannot consider them for this contest." I only knew they were missing out on Portland Wrestling – one of the best independent wrestling circuits of the day. I sent the same pictures to Bill Apter at Pro Wrestling Illustrated in New York City. Two weeks later he called an offered me a job taking pictures for him. That ignorance is bliss resulted in a 10-year assignment, paying me thousands of dollars to photograph some of the most exciting events in my life. Bill and I are friends today on Facebook.

My singing career I owe to Kathy Griffin. She sang a theme song for a short-lived talk show on Bravo a few years back. I loved the song and immediately bought it on iTunes. When I got ready to launch Rated G Radio, I wanted to write and sing a theme song my show! I hadn't sung since 6th grade choir, honestly could not carry a tune to save my life, and had zero knowledge of how to write a song or go about recording it. Then I said to myself, "Self, 6 months ago, you didn't even have a radio show or know how to do that!" With the ignorance is bliss enthusiasm, I asked people until I was finally connected with my producer, Brian Pothier, who told me before I sang my first off-key note, "I've worked with worse, so don't worry kid..." That was good enough for me! Today I'm an award winning singer-songwriter with #1 hit records on indie radio for over 60 consecutive weeks and was named "Hottest New Artist" by the HNA Network for 2017, and "Pop Artist of the Year" by the IMEA in 2016.

Yes, it's great to have the support of your family, friends, co-workers and everyone else on social media. Remember, though, it doesn't really matter if they believe in your dreams or not. It's only important if *you* do. If you want to be a rock star at 45 – do it! The clock is ticking. Make it happen! If you want to write that next great American novel – there are eager readers waiting for you! Whatever it is you want to do – take that first step today and do it now!

THE ISM TO REMEMBER:
You can do everything, if you think you can.

BLOND JESUS-ISM 9:
I'm Going To Rule The World When I Grow Up

BLOND JESUS-ISM #10

It's Going To Be Ok!

THE ISM OF 10:
Good or bad, if you dwell on it, you'll make everyone else dwell on it too. Choose your dwelling carefully.

PALPABLE PARABLE:
Do you remember your first crush? Sure you do. It was the cute Darla two rows up to your right in 7th period English. Your teacher, Mrs. Wilson, wore enough rose petal perfume to overpower the local florist. It gave you migraine headaches during the springtime when the weather is warm. Your hormones are in full bloom. And your thoughts are less on dangling participles than on what Darla is wearing and you're wondering if she's wondering about you.

Mrs. Wilson catches you drifting off into the sunset reminds your classmates, while sternly looking at you, "You have 10 minutes left on today's quiz. Make every minute count!"

You have much bigger problems than writing paragraph responses to her questions on Walt Whitman. The big dance is in two weeks! All of your friends seem to have found a date, except you. You still haven't gotten up the nerve to ask Darla to be your date. Trouble is, you've never been on a date before. Your older brother tells you just to "grow a pair" and while you're not sure entirely what that means, you do know he wants you to stop talking in your sleep about Darla.

"When I was your age..." he begins, forgetting how daunting it was, now an apparent dating guru's just 3 years your elder, "I had a date lined up for the Spring Formal weeks before now! What are you waiting for?!"

You're sure in the last 3 years the rules of dating have completely changed. Besides, that was so long ago, how does he even remember what it was like in 2014 anyway? You roll your eyes at your brothers ill fitting attempts to push you into "the ask." Yet, you listen with every ounce of concentration you can muster in hopes you'll end up picking up something, anything, that could be useful in helping you score the date with Darla.

Time was running out. You've heard rumors in the lunch room that your friends' friend, who goes to another school, and who is way more popular than you could ever hope to be, is also interested in Darla and he was going to ask her to the dance, too.

"I bet that other guy is way more cool, hip, pretty, handsome, fit, richer with cooler parents," you tell yourself.

Little do you know, this other mystery friend of a friend may have made this up, heard it wrong, or, better yet, is a real human, just like you, with real doubt and who is just as nervous as you are, if he is, indeed, also interested in Darla.

Friday afternoon arrives faster than you'd expected, but you're still stifled by Mrs. Wilson's stench. You're checking the clock. 2:27. Once the bell rings at 2:35 there would be a mad dash to the lockers, and then to catch the school bus home. There wouldn't be much time for date chat. Your window of opportunity is now!

The buzzer rings and you call out to Darla, "Hey – hold on…" Your friends smile as they push by you knowing you're about to lay it all on the line. You grab your notebook, cram it into your backpack, and nervously walk over. "The big dance is coming up in a couple weeks and I was wondering…" You stall for a moment hoping Darla will finish your sentence – like fate bringing two star-crossed lovers together in destiny. …"If you'd like to go with me. Be, my, um, date?"

Darla smiles back at you and without hesitation, "Sure. Sounds like fun. I gotta go or I'll miss my bus. Snapchat me later." Darla turns and heads out the door along with another 100 students anxious to begin their weekend.

Time stands still for that moment. Did Darla just say yes? What do I do now? What am I going to wear? Do we go to dinner first? I wonder if we have to go to someplace fancy, or can we just hit Taco Bell on the way there? I hope I don't sweat too much. I have got to bring breath mints – just in case.   I've only got

2 weeks and I don't even know how to dance.
Who can teach me to dance? What are we
going to talk about? Will be hold hands? Does
this make us a couple? Are we going steady?

All of these thoughts crowd your brain in the
next minute. Your friends come back into the
classroom and see the smile on your face.
"Looks like you got your answer... Now let's get
outta here." Your friends put their arm around
your shoulder and you push open the doors
and walk down the steps like you've just won
an Olympic gold medal.

Over the next week you run through your brain
at least a million times what you'll say, what
you'll eat, how you'll dance – both fast and
slow, what you'll wear, and practice how you'll
end the night – hopefully with a goodnight kiss.
You've even Snapchatted back and forth with
Darla to make sure the haze of Mrs. Wilson's
perfume didn't leave you hallucinating the
whole thing! Young love appears to be
blooming like springtime flowers. Everything
in the world seems happier and perfect. The
skies are bluer! Yes, life is perfect! You're now
actually talking to Darla between class and
things are looking good for the dance!

It's now Wednesday. Two days until the big date. You and your friends have been talking about what you're going to do before the dance on Friday. You've even figured out transportation. You've begged your parents to take you in your dads BMW. It would be worth the extra month of doing the dishes not to be seen going to pick up your first date in the maroon minivan your mom uses to get groceries and take you and your friends to soccer practice. Instead you tell your friends how your Dad wanted to take you in the BMW to really impress her.

After lunch when you and your friends are walking outside on campus, you see Darla talking to friends and something seems odd. You can't really put your finger on it, but something feels different from the fun texts you exchanged last night after doing your homework before bed. In English, Darla is acting weird. You think, "Well, it's probably nerves. I'm nervous, too." Something tells you its more than just nerves. And you know it's more than just the lack of air conditioning and ventilation in Mrs. Wilson's class that was making everyone nauseous.

After class, Darla quickly finds her friends and race off to the bus home. After you get home and turn your phone over to your mom, you get your homework done enjoy dinner with your family – your mom made her famous grilled chicken and quinoa salad, one of your recent favorites. When you get your phone back after doing the dishes, you've got a bunch of texts from your friends, but one stands out. A single text from Darla, "Hey, I can't go to the dance with you on Friday. Something came up. Sorry."

A couple of your friends text you, who just got Snapchatted by Darla's friends friends sister's cousin who knows this guy… Turns out she just got asked earlier that day by the mysterious BMOC (Big Man on Campus) and decided going with someone more popular and high profile was more important than going do THE DANCE of ALL TIME with you.

The shock turns to terror as you use your best inside voice to scream as loud as you possibly can, "No. NO. NO! This can't be happening. It's two days until the dance and now you are going to be the only one in human history who doesn't have a date to the dance! I can't ever go back to school. I can never show my face in

Mrs. Wilson's English class ever again. I might as well run away to Canada and join the French Foreign Legion at this point. I can't believe this is happening to MEEEEEEE!"

Your mind continues racing like your hamster on the habitrail wheel, to the point your mom even comments how distracted you were washing the dishes after dinner. "Honey, you know you need to actually put the dishes in the sink, scrub them with the sponge, then rinse them off, dry them with a towel, before putting them back in the cupboard. Going from the table to the cupboard and skipping everything in the middle is taking too many shortcuts, even for me."

"Sorry, mom. I'll rewash everything."

Shocked at this grand apology, your mom races over to you, feels your forehead for fever.

"What is going on with you?!?! I've never heard you volunteer to rewash the dishes! What's happened? Who died?"

"It's nothing. Just that, well, I can't ever go back to school. And, I'm probably going to have to leave the country – like tonight –

and..."

"Whoa! Whoa! Whoa! Back up. What happened today?"

"Nothing. Nothing. Except my life is completely ruined. I'm such a loser, mom, and I don't know what I'm going to do. Darla texted me after I got home today and now can't go to The Dance with me on Friday. You know, like the day after tomorrow? Turns out, the BMOC asked her and now I'm the complete laughing stock of the entire school. Everyone will make fun of me. The ONLY person without a date! I definitely can't go to The Dance NOW, mom. And I can't ever show my face in Mrs. Wilson's English class. I'm definitely going to have to transfer schools. I've never been so completely humiliated in my entire life, and..."

With this Barbara Walters worthy confession, your mom spins you towards her, smiles a knowing smile, and gives you the biggest hug you ever remember her giving you.

"Mom... I... can't... breathe...."

"Good. Then you can't run away, when I tell you this story. Now sit."

She pulls up a bar stool from the counter and you comply with her command.

"When I was your age…"

"Please, not another story about how you walked uphill in the snow to and from school every day of your school year when you lived at the beach in Santa Monica growing up…"

She smiles and continues, "When I was your age… I wanted this boy, Jerry Hart, to ask me to the Spring Formal. This was the big event at our school. All the boys would get new suits and all the girls would wear their prettiest dresses. I had a crush on Jerry all through my junior year. He was the star basketball player, was the most popular boy in school. All the boys wanted to be like Jerry. And all the girls wanted to graduate from high school and become Mrs. Jerry Hart. You should have seen my Pee-Chee folders. I'd write over and over and over, "Mr. & Mrs. Jerry Hart. I had it all planned in my head that we would go to the Spring Formal. And you know what happened?"

"You and Jerry went to the Spring Formal.."
you say, exasperated by the obvious.

"No, silly, Jerry asked my friend, Jennifer instead. Of course, Jennifer said 'yes' and I was crushed. I cried my eyes out for days. My mother, your grandmother, finally said, 'You have got to get ahold of yourself. No boy is worth all of this crying, moaning and wailing! Compose yourself, young lady, and start acting like one! Is he the only boy in your school?'"

Your mom grins. "I told Grandma that there was ONLY one Jerry Hart and I was sure I would never be able to go to school again, with my best friend in the whole world stabbing me in the back by going to the dance with him."

"What made it even worse, your Grandmother still made me go to the dance, without a date and I stood on the side of that stale gymnasium in my pretty yellow dress, hoping someone would come up to me and ask me to dance to Madonna's "Like A Virgin. Because at that moment in time, I was convinced that I would die a virgin and nobody would ever want to dance with me!"

"Mom… that's gross."

"Well, it's true, honey. And guess what. I went to that dance, by myself, and ended up hanging out with a bunch of other girls, and boys, who didn't have dates either. We had the best time slam dancing to the Clash's "Rock the Casbah" and afterwards we all went out for ice cream at Carvell's."

"And how does any of that apply to me? I'm the one who's been jilted two days before the dance!"

"You know your friend Matt? His parents, Christy and Rob met that same night. They didn't go with a date, and they found true love, and now you've got your friend Matt as living breathing proof, anything is possible."

"Oh mom…." You smile and roll your eyes, feeling somewhat better about your incredible tale of woe in life.

"So before you go rolling your eyes at me again, there are a stack of dishes waiting for you to actually get them wet with water and soap." She gives you a peck on the forehead and heads out to her Yoga class, "Be back by 8:00!"

You finish up rewashing dishes, making sure they are sparkling before carefully putting them back in the cupboards. You head to your room and Skype Matt.

"So you heard?"

"Heard what?"

"I got dumped for the dance..."

"I'm sorry to hear that. I don't have a date, either. Neither does Lisa or Corey. Come to think of it, there's a group of us who aren't paired up. We should all go together as a sign of unity being single!"

You laugh and suddenly you realize you're not alone in the world. As much as you thought you were the only person who "couldn't get a date" there are lots of other friends who don't have dates either. Inspired by this new information, you and Matt do a group Skype with everyone you can think of and organize all of your single classmates for Friday's dance.

Before you hang up, you smile into the computer to say, "Matt, thanks for being here for me. Oh, and by the way, Did I ever tell you about the time that your mom and dad met for the first time? I've got the inside scoop and it involves ice cream!"

FORTUITOUS FABLE:

It doesn't really matter what awful thing has presented itself to me over the years. Each time I was thrown under the bus or tossed into the fire or hacked up with knives in my back – the experiences were excruciating, horrific and, honestly at times left me feeling only what I can describe as something similar to what PTSD must be like. Yet here I am today, completing the last chapter in, what I hope will be, the first of many books.

Horrible things happen to everyone – not just you. In the previous chapters, I've shared with you different things that have happened in my life. Here, I'll breach a subject which few are willing to discuss. I'll share how these experiences in life did not, in fact, ruin my life, though at the time, it surely felt differently.

There are days when going through "emotional growth spurts" I'd have much rather stayed stunted, but that's not what life's about. These difficult times helped me evolve, develop, create, separate, flourish, blossom, reach, soar, climb, smile and be grateful once again. When you're going through one of these opportunities, remember to count your blessings and recognize there's a greater lesson to be learned – and look for the silver lining. Can you see it? Are there any obvious lessons you're being an ostrich on by burying your head in the sand?

I've been an ostrich many times, sometimes by choice, other times by ignorance. It happens.

So what's the topic, Garrett? What could you possibly share with us that will shock and dismay us from your already revealing secrets?

Barfing.

Yes, barfing. What a fun subject! Growing up, I was a barfer. It didn't matter if I were feeling sick, feeling happy, feeling nervous, feeling sleepy, feeling – whatever. Well, it did matter. I was nervous all the time. If I had reincarnated at that moment, I'd have been a Chihuahua! And, no, I did not have an eating disorder. It wasn't like I was going around looking to barf, it just happened. A lot. For some reason I was a nervous kid. Throwing up at school didn't happen "regularly" but looking back, I was the cause of a lot of the Pepto-Bismol smelling bark dust spread across the floors in my schools.

For the record, I'm sure there are additional scholastic barfing extravaganza's I've blocked from memory, but some of the standouts of my public barfing include:

- 4th Grade. Hayesville Elementary School. How does a tiny little stomach hold such a large volume of barf? It's scientifically impossible! More on science later. But this spring day, I would barf so much in the time the school called my mom to come pick me up and the time she arrived, I could have easily turned into a pile of dust from dehydration. I have no idea why anyone would want to be a school nurse. Dealing with barfing kids all the time. Gross!
- 7th Grade. First day of school! My dad dropped me off at Waldo Middle School and I no sooner made it in the doors, than I yacked all over the place. The school's secretary had to call my mom to come pick me up and drag me home. My mom gets an award for her BRS (Barfer Retrieval System). Gross!
- 9th Grade. I had a super bad migraine headache one spring afternoon – it was

so bad I had to be excused from 7th period science class. On my way to the exit not more than 20' away, I barfed all over the concrete stairs – right before class was out for the day, and it made a nice river-O-barf for everyone to navigate around as they tried to escape and go home. Gross!

- 10th Grade. First day of school. First period. Chemistry. 45 minutes earlier, while at home, I thought it would be a great idea to have unsweetened grapefruit juice for breakfast (on a nervous stomach, no less) before going to school. I get to the classroom and grab a desk with my buddy Jeff in the very front. We're chatting it up. As soon as the buzzer rings, and the teacher walks into the room I projectile vomit faster than Linda Blair can spin her head in the Exorcist. Twice. The teacher screams, "Run to the bathroom…" I did. And I puked some more. After emptying out the entire contents of my stomach, and then some, I showed my face back in class. "THE BARFER: RETURNS!" The chatter in the hallways the rest of the day centered on, "Did you hear

about the guy who barfed in Chemistry this morning?" And I'd go, "Gross!"
- President's Club, US West, Santa Fe, NM. Normally President's Club was held in exotic locations like Cancun or Hawaii or, well, someplace that wasn't Santa Fe, New Mexico. For this week of adventure and mayhem, I invited my Dad to go along with me. I was "newly single" at the time, and none of my friends could go with me on this all-expense paid vacation. Plus it was in Santa Fe, New Mexico. Listen, I think Santa Fe is a nice community – so save the letter writing campaign, but after working my ass off for the last 51 weeks, going to a desert location that didn't include snorkeling or swimming in the surf, well, just wasn't a President's Club to me.

At the Welcome Reception before dinner, complimentary food and beverage were graciously provided. Who needs food? Bring on the wine! I consumed lots of delicious Chardonnay and, I'm guessing, not a lot else. When I should have called it a night and headed back to my room to sleep it off, I wanted to get on a bus with all of my friends and head to the casino to gamble!

If you think you know what happens next, you're wrong! I didn't go to the casino and lose all of my money. Though I tried. Instead, I got on the shuttle bus, and about 2 blocks from the casino, puked my guts out inside the bus while trying to make the barf go out the window. Gross!

Nothing can be more embarrassing that barfing in public. In plain view or thinly-veiled, barfing sucks. I'm not sure what the "normal" amount of public barfing might be for one person in their lifetime, but I'm sure I've exceeded the quota. I like being an over achiever, even in dubious categories like public barfing.

In each of these barfing extravaganzas, I was absolutely sure my life would end at that moment. I would surely have to remove myself from society. Time would pass, yet there would always be talk of "The Barfer." None of that happened. What did? I pulled my head out of the porcelain, wiped my chin, brushed my teeth, and went back out with a smile on my face. Why? Because that's what you do in life when you barf.

Barfing my brains out in public was definitely not something I'm proud of doing. Each time it seemed like the most embarrassing thing I'd ever done. Each time. Think on the "each time" concept for a moment. More than once. This means entirely different sets of people saw me barf – and yet, after cleaning myself up, people still talked to me, still sat next to me in class, still worked with me. They were forgiving. And, what choice did I have? To flush the toilet with my head in the bowl? Of course not.

When life hands you a barfy situation, make the best of it. Get it all out as quickly as you can. It's short-term. When you've purged everything, clean yourself up, brush yourself off, and get back up and get out in the world.

You'll only be remembered as "The Barfer" if you want to be.

THE ISM TO REMEMBER:
Good or bad, if you dwell on it, you'll make everyone else dwell on it too. Choose your dwelling carefully.

BLOND JESUS-ISM 10:
You Are Going To Be Ok!

About
Garrett Miller

As diverse for his range of projects as he is for his commanding voice on radio, Garrett Miller is a singer, songwriter, and author who shares his messages of hope and inspiration with the world.

Born in Salem, Oregon, Garrett's eye for the creative started as a professional wrestling photographer in the 1980's. After a successful career in sales, Garrett created his own radio program in 2012, "Rated G Radio," featuring a wide range of award winning singers, actors and other interesting characters.

In 2013 Garrett recorded his first EP, "Eyes Wide" featuring the holiday classic, "Guess What Its Christmastime." He released the follow up full-length album, "Blond Jesus" in 2015 with radio friendly hits including, "Gay Wedding," "Sweat & Testify," "Witch Sisters Halloween," and the title track - which have been #1 hits on the indie music charts worldwide.

Garrett is currently acting in indie films and TV projects including "OPEN" "Old Dogs New Tricks", "Unfallen", "Ugly Sweater Party", and "Child of the 70's" among other releases.

www.ingramcontent.com/pod-product-compliance
Lightning Source LLC
Chambersburg PA
CBHW061654040426
42446CB00010B/1729